Advanced Concurrency Java

Dedicated to my wife Kamini

Author information

For any help please contact :
Amazon Author Page :
amazon.com/author/ajaykumar
Email : ajaycucek@gmail.com ,
ajaxreso@gmail.com
Linkedin :
https://www.linkedin.com/in/ajaycucek
Facebook :
https://www.facebook.com/ajaycucek
Youtube :
https://www.youtube.com/channel/UC1uXEe
btqCLYxVdzirKZGIA
Twitter : https://twitter.com/ajaycucek
Instagram :
https://www.instagram.com/ajaycucek/
Skype : ajaycucek

Table of contents

6

Book Overview

I know how scary the title of this book might look, but don't be afraid. I'll take you through it step by step. We will see the patterns, how things can go wrong, and how to deal with the situation. This book is divided into below mentioned modules.

- Introducing the Executor Pattern, Futures and Callables
- Using Locks and Semaphores for the Producer / Consumer Pattern
- Controlling Concurrent Applications Using Barriers and Latches
- Understanding Compare and Swap (CASing) and Atomic Variables
- Leveraging Concurrent Collections to Simplify Application Design

If you follow me, at the end of this book, you will have a good idea of the ExecutorService Patterns and callables, and futures, what is interruptible or timed out lock acquisition, what are logs, semaphores, barriers, and latches, and what is CASing, and atomic variables. And at last, we will see the concurrent collections, copy and write release, concurrent hashmaps, and concurrent skip lists. But before you move on, you would like to be familiar with the Java language and the collection API. You also need some knowledge of concurrency and be able to write basic lambda expressions. Yes, this is an ambitious ride, but don't be afraid. Just let me guide you through all this, and you will see that from the other side, concurrencies, in fact, not that scary.

Module 1: Introducing the Executor Pattern, Futures and Callables

Introduction, What are you going to learn in this book?

What is this book about? Well, this book is about advanced concurrency in Java, and mainly, how to improve the Runnable pattern in different ways. First, we will talk about the Executor pattern and the futures and callable. We will cover that in details. Then we will talk about the Java primitives introduced to synchronize tasks. Those primitives have been introduced in Java 5. We will then cover in details the compare and swap pattern and atomic variables. We will describe this concept very precisely. And we will finish by browsing the concurrent collections and maps introduced in the Collection Framework. In the module covering Java concurrent primitives, we will cover the lock and the semaphore, which are alternatives to the synchronized block patterns that we will use to implement the Producer/Consumer pattern. And we will also talk about barriers and latches and see the patterns to use them properly.

What Do You Need to Know to Follow This book?

Who are you and what do you need to know to follow this book? Well, this is, of course, a Java book, so you need to have a fair knowledge of the Java language and its main APIs. You should be able to use a standard IDE like Eclipse or IntelliJ or the life coding parts of this book will be made using Eclipse. You should know the Collection Framework quite well because we are going to use it quite a lot in this book. The Collection Framework is really a basic framework in all the Java applications, so you are probably already familiar with this framework. You also need to have at least some knowledge about concurrency. You should know the runnable pattern. You should be able to implement the Producer/Consumer pattern using the Wait/Notify pattern, and you should know what visibility and happens-before mean in concurrency in Java.

Introducing Executors, What Is Wrong with the Runnable Pattern?

Let us jump in the first part of the first module of this book about the Executor pattern. And first, let us take a look at this code.
Runnabletask= () -> System.out.println("Hello world!");

```
Threadthread= newThread(task);
thread.start();
```
This code is an example of the Runnable pattern in action. First, a task is an instance of the Runnable interface. Since this Runnable interface is a functional interface, we can implement it using a lambda expression. Then we create a new instance of a Thread class and pass this runnable as a parameter to the construction of this object. And then at last, we call the start method on this Thread object and this will have the effect of executing the runnable, thus this task, in a new thread. Now let us take a closer look at this pattern and try to understand what is wrong with it.

- A thread is created on demand, by the user
- Once the task is done, the thread dies
- Problem: a thread is an expensive resource...

The first point is that the thread is created on demand by the user. The user being a developer. Now the risk is that everybody can create new threads freely and you might end up with thousands of threads created in your application, thus killing it. This idea is not a great idea. Second, a new thread is created for each task, and when the task is done, the thread dies. This is how this start method works. The problem is that a thread might be a resource given by the operating system and we all know that these resources are expensive both to create and to kill. So in fact, this pattern, even if it works from a pure technical point of view is not that great and should not be used in real applications. In fact, if what you are developing is a Java EE application, you should not use it at all. In Java EE application, you are not allowed to create new threads on your own.

Defining the Executor Pattern: A New Pattern to Launch Threads

The first goal of the Executor pattern is to fix precisely these issues. So first of all, how can we improve the user threads as resources. Well, we can think about creating pools of ready-to-use threads, this is a very classical solution, and use them on demand. So instead of creating a new thread with each task as a parameter, we will create tasks as we did by implementing the Runnable interface and we are going to submit them to pools of threads that will execute it. It will be the role of the pool of threads to take a task, choose an available thread, pass this task to this thread, and execute it in this thread.

- We need (at least) two patterns:
  - The first one to create a pool of threads
  - The second one to pass a task to this pool

So we need at least two patterns, the first one is to create a pool of threads, and the second one to pass a task to this pool of threads.

Defining the Executor Service Pattern, a First Simple Example

In Java, a pool of thread is an instance of the Executor interface.

```java
public interface Executor {
void execute(Runnable task);
}
```
This Executor interface is very simple. It has only one method, execute, that takes a runnable task. We do not have to implement this interface ourselves. There are several implementations readily available in the JDK.
```java
public interface ExecutorService extends
Executor {
// 11 more methods
}
```
We have a second interface called the ExecutorService that extends Executor. ExecutorService has about 10 more methods than executor, but in fact, it turns out that all the implementations of Executor are also implementations of ExecutorService. The implementations are the same for both interfaces. To create instances of those implementations, we have a factory class called Executors with an S with about 20 methods to create executors. For instance, let us build a pool of thread with only one thread in it.
```java
ExecutorService singleThreadExecutor =
Executors.newSingleThreadExecutor();
```
We can use the newSingleThreadExecutor factory method from the Executors class. How does this pool of thread works? In fact, when we create it, this thread is created also and will be kept alive as long as this pool of thread is alive. Then, when we pass a task to this ExecutorService, this task will be executed in that thread and this thread will not be destroyed once this task is done. It brings the question of how are we going to free the threads of this ExecutorService. In fact, on ExecutorService, there is a set of shutdown

method that we are going to see at the end of this part.

Comparing the Runnable and the Executor Service Patterns

We are not going to see all of the methods from the Executors factory class. We will see several examples in the java coding part of this module. The two most used methods from this class are the following. The first one is the newSingleThreadExecutor that is used to create a pool of thread with only one thread in it. It is very useful for reactive programming when you just want to execute a single task in another thread. And the second one is the FixedThreadPoolExecutor.
ExecutorServicen multipleThreadsExecutor= Executors.newFixedThreadPoolExecutor(8);
It is a pool of thread in which you can fix the number of thread, 8, in this example. Alright, so we can create an executor on a single thread, then create a runnable task as we just did, and pass this task to the executor.
Executor executor= Executors.newSingleThreadExecutor();
Runnable task= () -> System.out.println("I run!");
executor.execute(task);
What is going to happen, the executor will take this task, take its only thread since it has only one, and execute this task in the thread. When this task is done, then the thread will be available to execute another task.
// Executor pattern
executor.execute(task);

```
// Runnable pattern
newThread(task).start();
```
So we can compare those two patterns. In the first one, we pass the task to the Executor. In the second one, we pass the task to a new instance of Thread. So basically, the Executor pattern does not create a new thread and this is exactly what we wanted to do, but the behavior is the same. Both calls the execute method call and the start method call will return immediately and the task will be executed in another thread sometime in the future.

Understanding the Waiting Queue of the Executor Service

```
Executor executor=
Executors.newSingleThreadExecutor();
Runnable task1= () ->
someReallyLongProcess();
Runnable task2= () ->
anotherReallyLongProcess();
executor.execute(task1);
executor.execute(task2);
```
Now suppose we run this code. We create an Executor on the single thread, create a first task which will take some time to execute, and a second task which will also take some time to execute, and we submit those two tasks to the same Executor. So obviously, task2 will have to wait for task1 to be done. So to handle this case, an Executor, whether it is single threaded or not, has to waiting queue. Now this waiting queue is precisely specified. How does it work? First, a task is added to the

waiting queue when no thread is available. So suppose we have an ExecutorService built on full thread and all the threads are busy. If a new task is submitted, it will be added to this waiting queue. The second rule is that the tasks are executed in the order of their submission. So in our example, we have the guarantee that task1 will be executed before task2. This is very important in ordering our tasks. But of course, more questions can be asked. First, can we know if a task is done or not. Second question, can we cancel the execution of a task. The answer to the first question is no. In fact, in this case, when we are using runnable, it is not possible to query the Executor to know if a given task is executed or not. Second, can we cancel the execution of the task. In a certain way, we can. In fact, what we can do is remove a task from the waiting queue. If the task has been started by the thread, it is not possible to cancel it.

Wrapping-up the Executor Service Pattern

Okay, so let us quickly wrap up what we saw on the Executor pattern. First of all, building an executor is more efficient than creating threads on demand. Creating an Executor or ExecutorService will create a pool of thread when this Executor is created and those threads will remain alive as long as the executor is alive. So one given thread can execute as many tasks as we need. Second, we can pass instances of Runnable to an Executor. The Executor has a waiting queue

16

to handle the fact that it can have more requests than available threads. And if we want, we can ask the Executor to remove a task from the waiting queue. So as we can see, using the Executor pattern is more efficient than using the basic Runnable pattern and it is not incompatible with the runnable pattern since it can use the same tasks.

From Runnable to Callable: What Is Wrong with Runnables?

Now that we saw how to create pools of threads in the JDK using the Executor pattern, let us take a closer look at the runnable interface itself. So we saw that we could model a task to be executed in another thread using the runnable interface. Now there are several caveats in this runnable interface.

- A task does not return anything
  - No object can be returned
  - No exception can be raised
- There is no way we can know if a task is done or not

First, the method we write cannot return anything. And what does it mean? It mean first that no object can be returned and that no exception can be raised. Suppose our task involved some kind of database querying. A database query is something we might want to execute in another thread because it can be a long-running process. This query can go longer and the standard way to tell that in the JDK is to throw a SQL exception, and if it goes well, it will simply produce a result. This result or this exception cannot be transmitted through the Runnable task. In fact, there is no way we can know if a task is done or not, if it has complete normally or exceptionally, and this task cannot produce any result.

Defining a New Model for Tasks That Return Objects

So we have several questions. First of all, how can a task return value? Second question, how can we get the exceptions raised by this task and we can think about the IU exception or the SQL exception, for instance. And third, we need a way to transmit this value or the exception from one thread to another. Why? Because a task is created in a given thread, passed to a thread of an ExecutorService, and it is in this last thread that the result of the exception is created. So we need a new model for our tasks. What is okay with the runnable interface is that a task is a method of an interface, but this method has to return a value and must be able to throw an exception. It is not the case of the run method of the runnable interface. And we also need a new object that will act as a bridge between the executing thread belonging to the Executor and the main thread in which the task is created.

Introducing the Callable Interface to Model Tasks

```
@FunctionalInterface
public interface Runnable{
void run();
}
```

If we take a look at the Runnable interface, it is written like that with a single run method that does not return anything and that does not throw any exception. Now the Executor pattern uses another interface called the Callable interface.

```
@FunctionalInterface
public interface Callable<V>{
V call() throws Exception;
}
```

The Callable interface is a generate interface. It has a single method just as the Runnable interface called call. This call method returns an object of type V and may throw an Exception, so it does exactly what we need. As we saw the Executor interface does not handle callable directly. It has a single method that takes a runnable as a parameter. But the ExecutorService interface has a submit method that takes a callable as a parameter.

```
<T> Future<T> submit(Callable<T>task);
```

So to use callable tasks, we have to use ExecutorServices instead of Executors. Now as we saw in the previous part, the implementations of the ExecutorServices are the same as the implementations of the Executor interface and this method returns a future object that is also a generic object. In fact, this object is a wrapper on the object returned by the task, but it has also special functionalities that we are going to see.

Introducing the Future Object to Transmit Objects Between Threads

How does this future object work? Well, suppose that we create a callable in the main thread. This is the task we want to execute in the Executor we have, so we pass this task to the submit method of this Executor. This task is then transmitted from the main thread to the ExecutorService. Now the ExecutorService is going to execute it in a thread of its own pool, which is of course, different from the main thread. This special thread will create a result whether it is a normal result or an exception. Then the Executor will have to pass this object from its thread to the main thread that created the task. This is precisely the role of this Future object. In fact, the Executor will return a Future object that is going to hold the result of the execution of this task once it is available. How does it work in the code?

```
// In the main thread
Callable<String> task= () ->
buildPatientReport();
Future<String> future=
executor.submit(task);
String result= future.get();
```

I create the task in the main thread, then submit this task, and this submit method will immediately return a Future object with the same type as the type of the callable. Then I can call the get method on this Future object. I can execute some other code before calling this get method. What happens when I call this get method, two things can happen. First, the object produced by the task is available, so the get method will return that object immediately, and second, the object produced by the task is not yet available. In that case, the get method will not return immediately. It will block until the string in our example is available.

Wrapping-up Callables and Futures, Handling Exceptions

Now if things go wrong, two exceptions can be raised. First, the InterruptedException. This exception is thrown if the thread from the Executor that is executing this task has been interrupted. It is possible to interrupt such a thread by issuing a shutdown command to the Executor. The second case is that the task itself has thrown an exception. Imagine a query on a database and there has been some kind of error, so a SQL exception has been raised in the task internally. Then in that case, the get method will wrap this root exception in an ExecutionException and throw it in the main thread. So in a nutshell, this get method may throw two kinds of exception, InterruptedException, meaning that something went wrong in the Executor itself, or ExecutionException to wrap an application exception thrown by the task. So the future.get method works in that way. First case, the task completed normally, then the get method will return the produced result immediately if it is

21

available, if it is not the case, the get method will block until the result is ready. Second case, the get method threw an exception. Then this exception is wrapped in an ExecutionException and thrown by the get call. And there is also another possibility, we can also pass a timeout to the get call to avoid to be blocked indefinitely. So for instance, if we think that the result should be made available in less than a second, we can pass 1 second to this get method and pass the time the get method will throw an InterruptedException.

Java Coding: Introduction, Runnable in Action

Okay, time for a little java coding session. Let us see some code in action. What are we going to see in this java coding session? Well, we are going to create simple tasks and submit them to an Executor and see what happens in all the cases that we talked about. We also pass result through futures and see what happens when things go wrong, play with exceptions, and play with timeouts. So let us first have a look at how Executors and ExecutorServices work in Java.

```
package executors;
public class
PlayingWithExecutorsAndRunnables {
    public static void main(String[] args) {
        Runnable task = () ->
System.out.println("I am in thread " +
Thread.currentThread().getName());
        for (int i = 0 ; i < 10 ; i++) {
```

```
            new Thread(task).start();
        }
    }
}
```
Output at console :
I am in thread Thread-0
I am in thread Thread-2
I am in thread Thread-1
I am in thread Thread-4
I am in thread Thread-7
I am in thread Thread-5
I am in thread Thread-3
I am in thread Thread-8
I am in thread Thread-9
I am in thread Thread-6
We have created a task instance of Runnable, very simple, and implemented using lambda. What does this task do? It just print out a message as we're going to see on the console that is there to show the name of the thread executing this task. Let us create a Thread to run this task and start it. If we execute this code, it prints I am in Thread-0, which is the name of the thread executing this task. Now if I am executing this task 10 times, let us see what happens. I can see that every time a new thread is created, 0, 5, 6, the 1 is there, the 2 is there, etc, the Java virtual machine has created 10 threads here just because this is exactly what I asked for and those 10 different threads have executed this task and then have been destroyed.

Java Coding: Executor and Callables, How to Shut Down an Executor

```java
package executors;
import java.util.concurrent.ExecutorService;
import java.util.concurrent.Executors;
public class
PlayingWithExecutorsAndRunnables {
    public static void main(String[] args) {
        Runnable task = () ->
System.out.println("I am in thread " +
Thread.currentThread().getName());
        ExecutorService service =
Executors.newSingleThreadExecutor();
        for (int i = 0 ; i < 10 ; i++) {
            // new Thread(task).start();
            service.execute(task);
        }
        service.shutdown();
    }
}
```

Output at console :
I am in thread pool-1-thread-1
I am in thread pool-1-thread-1
I am in thread pool-1-thread-1
I am in thread pool-1-thread-1
I am in thread pool-1-thread-1
I am in thread pool-1-thread-1
I am in thread pool-1-thread-1
I am in thread pool-1-thread-1
I am in thread pool-1-thread-1
I am in thread pool-1-thread-1
Now let us take a look at the same code built
on an ExecutorService. So let us create an
ExecutorService, ExecutorService, and I am

24

going to use the factory class, Executors.newSingleThreadExecutor, and instead of launching my task by creating a thread every time, I am going to use this service, service.Execute, and pass this runnable as a parameter. Now if I execute this code, I can see that all the tasks have been executed in the same thread one at a time in this ExecutorService. There is also another detail I should mention is the fact that here I can see that the Java virtual machine that is executing my test is still alive. It has not been shut down. Why? Because this service is still alive, I did not shut it down, and since they are non-deamon threads in it, it maintains the Java virtual machine alive. So I need to add this code for my application to be correct, shutdown on this ExecutorService. Let us now run this code. All my tasks have been executed in the same thread and this time the virtual machine has been properly shut down. Now let us change this ExecutorService.

```
package executors;
import java.util.concurrent.ExecutorService;
import java.util.concurrent.Executors;
public class PlayingWithExecutorsAndRunnables {
    public static void main(String[] args) {
        Runnable task = () -> System.out.println("I am in thread " + Thread.currentThread().getName());
        // ExecutorService service = Executors.newSingleThreadExecutor();
        ExecutorService service = Executors.newFixedThreadPool(4);
        for (int i = 0 ; i < 10 ; i++) {
            // new Thread(task).start();
            service.execute(task);
        }
```

```
        service.shutdown();
    }
}
```
Output at console :
I am in thread pool-1-thread-2
I am in thread pool-1-thread-4
I am in thread pool-1-thread-1
I am in thread pool-1-thread-3
I am in thread pool-1-thread-4
I am in thread pool-1-thread-2
I am in thread pool-1-thread-4
I am in thread pool-1-thread-3
I am in thread pool-1-thread-1
I am in thread pool-1-thread-2
Let us comment out this code, and instead of creating a single thread ExecutorService, let us create a fixed thread ExecutorService with four threads in it and let us execute the exact same code. I can see now that all my tasks have been executed in their own threads, thread-1, thread-2, 3, and 4. ExecutorServices work. You create one, you do not forget to shut it down, and we saw several strategies to do that in the previous pages, and they are going to execute your tasks in their threads and we'll be able to reuse them as needed.

Java Coding: Using Futures to Handle Time Out

Now let us see what happens if a task takes too much time to produce its result.
package executors;
import java.util.concurrent.Callable;
import java.util.concurrent.ExecutionException;

26

```java
import java.util.concurrent.ExecutorService;
import java.util.concurrent.Executors;
import java.util.concurrent.Future;
public class PlayingWithCallablesAndFutures
{
    public static void main(String[] args)
throws ExecutionException,
InterruptedException {
        Callable<String> task = () -> {
            Thread.sleep(300);
            return "I am in thread " +
Thread.currentThread().getName();
        };
        ExecutorService executor =
Executors.newFixedThreadPool(4);
        for (int i = 0; i < 10; i++) {
            Future<String> future =
executor.submit(task);
            System.out.println("I get: " +
future.get());
        }
        executor.shutdown();
    }
}
```
Output at console :
I get: I am in thread pool-1-thread-1
I get: I am in thread pool-1-thread-2
I get: I am in thread pool-1-thread-3
I get: I am in thread pool-1-thread-4
I get: I am in thread pool-1-thread-1
I get: I am in thread pool-1-thread-2
I get: I am in thread pool-1-thread-3
I get: I am in thread pool-1-thread-4
I get: I am in thread pool-1-thread-1
I get: I am in thread pool-1-thread-2
Let us simulate that by adding here
Thread.sleep and pass, for instance, 300 ms. If
we run this code, we see that obviously it takes
some time for all the task to be executed. Now

if we cannot wait a very long time, we saw that it is possible to pass a timeout to this get future. Let us do that with 100 ms TimeUnit.MILLISECONDS.

```java
package executors;
import java.util.concurrent.Callable;
import java.util.concurrent.ExecutionException;
import java.util.concurrent.ExecutorService;
import java.util.concurrent.Executors;
import java.util.concurrent.Future;
import java.util.concurrent.TimeUnit;
import java.util.concurrent.TimeoutException;
public class PlayingWithCallablesAndFutures
{
    public static void main(String[] args)
throws ExecutionException,
InterruptedException, TimeoutException {
        Callable<String> task = () -> {
            Thread.sleep(300);
            return "I am in thread " +
Thread.currentThread().getName();
        };
        ExecutorService executor =
Executors.newFixedThreadPool(4);
        for (int i = 0; i < 10; i++) {
            Future<String> future =
executor.submit(task);
            System.out.println("I get: " +
future.get(100, TimeUnit.MILLISECONDS));
        }
        executor.shutdown();
    }
}
```

Output at console :
Exception in thread "main"
java.util.concurrent.TimeoutException

28

at
java.util.concurrent.FutureTask.get(Unknown Source)
        at
executors.PlayingWithCallablesAndFutures.main(PlayingWithCallablesAndFutures.java:19)
This get method is not the same as the previous one, and now it can throw a timeout exception. So let us hide this throw closer to our one main method and let us run this code again. Obviously, no task has the chance to be executed, so the concurrent TimeoutException will be thrown. Now we can see that once again, the JVM that run our little test did not shut down properly, so let us do that manually. Why so? Because this get method threw the exception and did not let this shutdown method to be executed. So for this code to be correct, we need to wrap it in a try, finally, close them just like that.

```
package executors;
import java.util.concurrent.Callable;
import
java.util.concurrent.ExecutionException;
import java.util.concurrent.ExecutorService;
import java.util.concurrent.Executors;
import java.util.concurrent.Future;
import java.util.concurrent.TimeUnit;
import
java.util.concurrent.TimeoutException;
public class PlayingWithCallablesAndFutures
{
    public static void main(String[] args)
throws ExecutionException,
InterruptedException, TimeoutException {
        Callable<String> task = () -> {
            Thread.sleep(300);
            return "I am in thread " +
Thread.currentThread().getName();
```

```
        };
        ExecutorService executor =
Executors.newFixedThreadPool(4);
        try {
            for (int i = 0; i < 10; i++) {
                Future<String> future =
executor.submit(task);
                System.out.println("I get: "
+ future.get(100,
TimeUnit.MILLISECONDS));
            }
        } finally {
            executor.shutdown();
        }
    }
}
```

Now if I execute this code again, I can see that my Java machine has been properly shut down as this executor.shutdown has been executed, even if this get method threw the exception.

Java Coding: Handling Exceptions in Callables with Futures

And last thing I would like to show you is the following, the task that does not complete properly and that throws an exception.

```
package executors;
import java.util.concurrent.Callable;
import
java.util.concurrent.ExecutionException;
import java.util.concurrent.ExecutorService;
import java.util.concurrent.Executors;
import java.util.concurrent.Future;
```

```java
public class PlayingWithCallablesAndFutures
{
    public static void main(String[] args)
    throws ExecutionException,
    InterruptedException {
        Callable<String> task = () -> {
            throw new
IllegalStateException("I throw an exception in
thread " +
Thread.currentThread().getName());
        };
        ExecutorService executor =
Executors.newFixedThreadPool(4);
        for (int i = 0; i < 10; i++) {
            Future<String> future =
executor.submit(task);
            System.out.println("I get: " +
future.get());
        }
executor.shutdown();
    }
}
```

Output at console :
Exception in thread "main"
java.util.concurrent.ExecutionException:
java.lang.IllegalStateException: I throw an
exception in thread pool-1-thread-1
    at
java.util.concurrent.FutureTask.report(Unkn
own Source)
    at
java.util.concurrent.FutureTask.get(Unknown
Source)
    at
executors.PlayingWithCallablesAndFutures.m
ain(PlayingWithCallablesAndFutures.java:16)
Caused by: java.lang.IllegalStateException: I
throw an exception in thread pool-1-thread-1

at executors.PlayingWithCallablesAndFutures.lambda$0(PlayingWithCallablesAndFutures.java:10)
		at java.util.concurrent.FutureTask.run(Unknown Source)
		at java.util.concurrent.ThreadPoolExecutor.runWorker(Unknown Source)
		at java.util.concurrent.ThreadPoolExecutor$Worker.run(Unknown Source)
		at java.lang.Thread.run(Unknown Source)

Here, I've created a task that throws an IllegalStateException. It could have been any other exception. And I have the same code here that we'll call the get method on this future object. What is going to happen, let us run this code, here I can see that in my main thread on the get method here, Line 23, I have this Java.util.concurrent.ExecutionException that is thrown by this get method. This ExecutionException is always the same and it is caused by, so it means that this ExecutionException has a root exception associated to it. Thus this message caused by IllegalStateException, I throw an exception in thread pool-1-thread-, and this is the root exception thrown from inside my callable with the stack trays that leads to the right line of this callable here, Line 16 of my code.

Now compare the above code and output with below code and output

```
package executors;
public class PlayingWithNormalException {
	public static void main(String[] args){
		callMe();
```

32

```java
    }
    private static void callMe() {
        throw new IllegalStateException("I
throw an exception in thread " +
Thread.currentThread().getName());
    }
}
```

Output at console :

Exception in thread "main"
java.lang.IllegalStateException: I throw an
exception in thread main
        at
executors.PlayingWithNormalException.call
Me(PlayingWithNormalException.java:7)
        at
executors.PlayingWithNormalException.main
(PlayingWithNormalException.java:4)

Once again, I have to notice that in class
PlayingWithCallablesAndFutures.java this
get method prevented by JVM to close
properly, so I need to wrap this code in a try
and finally closer to be sure that my
application will properly terminate even in
that case.

```java
package executors;
import java.util.concurrent.Callable;
import
java.util.concurrent.ExecutionException;
import java.util.concurrent.ExecutorService;
import java.util.concurrent.Executors;
import java.util.concurrent.Future;
public class PlayingWithCallablesAndFutures
{
    public static void main(String[] args)
throws ExecutionException,
InterruptedException {
        Callable<String> task = () -> {
            throw new
IllegalStateException("I throw an exception in
```

```java
                thread " +
Thread.currentThread().getName());
        };
        ExecutorService executor =
Executors.newFixedThreadPool(4);
        try {
            for (int i = 0; i < 10; i++) {
                Future<String> future =
executor.submit(task);
                System.out.println("I get: "
+ future.get());
            }
        } finally {
            executor.shutdown();
        }
    }
}
```

Java Coding Wrap-up

Let us quickly wrap up this java coding
session. What did we see? Well, first we saw
how to pass tasks to Executors, whether they
are runnables that do not produce any results
or callables that do produce results, we saw
how to properly shutdown an Executor, and
this is really important, because the threads of
an Executor are not diamond threads, so they
will prevent JVM to exit properly, if not, shut
down. We saw how to pass an object created
in a callable to the main thread or at least to
the thread that created this callable and we
also saw how to handle problematic behaviors,
first callables that take too much time to
execute through the use of timeouts on the
Future object and how to handle application

exception from within a callable, once again, through the Future object.

Wrapping-up Executors: Single, Fixed, and Cached ExecutorServices

Let us talk now a little more about available ExecutorServices. When we built our first Executors, I told you that there was this Executors factory class with a bunch of methods to create Executors. We are not going to present all of them one by one, but we are going to see the categories of Executors we have. So as I told you, the JDK comes with several ExecutorServices available. The first we saw is the newSingleThreadExecutor.

- newSingleThreadExecutor()
  - an executor with only one thread

It is a special executor with only one thread in it.

- newFixedThreadPool(poolSize)
  - an executor with poolSizethreads

And the second one is a FixedThreadPool Executor that we can create with this method and pass the number threads we want in it.

- newCachedThreadPool()
  - creates threads on demand
  - keeps unused threads for 60s
  - then terminates them

We also have CachedThreadPools. Those CachedThreadPools differed from the FixedThreadPools in a way that those executors create threads on demand. This is different from the FixedThreadPool. The FixedThreadPool, if created with four threads, will create those four threads immediately. The CachedThreadPool create those threads on demand and will keep them for a certain amount of time. Now if the thread created are not used for 60 seconds by default, then this thread pool will destroy them. This kind of pool is very efficient if you have from time to time an important number of tasks to execute, but it turns out that you do not have to do that very often, for instance, once in several hours. So you can create the thread pool. It will not consume many resources since most of the time it will not have any threads at all, but when you need those threads, it will create them for you.

Wrapping-up Executors: Scheduled ExecutorService

- newScheduledThreadPool(poolSize)
    - creates a pool of threads
    - returns a ScheduledExecutorService

And a fourth and last factory method that we see is the newScheduledThreadPool. It returns a special ExecutorService that is in fact an extension of the ExecutorService interface called the ScheduledExecutorService. What does this special executor do?

- schedule(task, delay)
- scheduleAtFixedRate(task, delay, period)
- scheduleWithFixedDelay(task, initialDelay, delay)

Well, it does three things. First, I can schedule a task somewhere in the future by passing this task and a delay, which is a special amount of time. Then I can call scheduleAtFixedRate. It will execute this task after a certain delay and then execute it again and again after a certain period of time. So this task will be executed indefinitely starting in 5 minutes, and for instance, every 30 seconds. And the last method is scheduleWithFixedDelay. At a first glimpse, it works the same as the previous method. It takes an initalDelay and then a second delay which acts as a period. In fact, it does not work exactly the same. This task will be first executed after the initial delay and then executed again after a certain delay. The second delay is measured between the end of the execution of this task and the beginning of the next execution of this task.

Shutting Down an ExecutorService: Patterns and Strategies

Okay, so let us now cover the last point of this first module, How to Shut down an ExecutorService. This is something we briefly mentioned at the beginning of this module and it is now time to see that. As we saw, an ExecutorService is a pool of threads that needs to be properly shut down as any system resource opened in an application. There are three methods basically to shut down an ExecutorService. First, the shutdown method.

- shutdown()

- continue to execute all submitted tasks
- execute waiting tasks
- do not accept new tasks-then shutdown

It will continue to execute all submitted tasks including the tasks that are still waiting in the waiting queue. Once an ExecutorService has been shut down, it will not accept any new tasks. And when all the tasks have complete, then it will shut down properly destroying and cleaning up all the threads that have been created. This is the soft way of closing an ExecutorService respectful of everything that has been submitted to it. Of course, if you needed to shut down an ExecutorService quickly, you might not be able to wait for all the tasks to complete. So there is a second method for that, shutdownNow.

- shutdownNow()
  - halt the running tasks
  - do not execute waiting tasks
  - then shutdown

This method will halt the running tasks, interrupting the threads that are executing them. It will not execute any waiting tasks. Of course, it will not allow any new submission and then it will shut down. This shutdownNow method is the hard way of shutting down an ExecutorService. It is not respectful of the running tasks since it will hold them immediately. There is a third way between the first and the second one, the wait termination that takes a timeout as a parameter.

- awaitTermination(timeout)
  - shutdown()
  - wait for the timeout
  - if there are remaining tasks, then halt everything

First, it will issue a shutdownNow, so it will prevent the submission of any new task, then it will wait for the given timeout. During this timeout, it gives the chance of all the executing tasks to complete and of all the waiting tasks to be executed, and at the end of this timeout, if there are still remaining tasks, it will halt everything and cleanup the waiting queue if it is not empty.

Module Wrap-up

Well, now is the time to wrap up this module. So what did we learn in this module? First of all, we saw that allowing developers to create threads on demand in an application might not be such a great idea and we saw how to create pools of threads through the ExecutorService pattern, which is much better. Then we saw that the runnable interface is a nice model for tasks to be executed in other threads, but we also have the callable model which is much better, which allows a task to produce results. We saw how to submit Callables to ExecutorServices and how to get results whether normal or exceptional results produced by those Callables. And we saw how to properly handle exceptions. There are two kinds of exceptions. Exceptions normally created by a task all thrown by the pool of thread itself. And at last, we saw how to properly shutdown executors, which is not as simple as it may seem.

Module 2: Using Locks and Semaphores for the Producer / Consumer Pattern

Introduction, Module Agenda

This module is about synchronization. Now we have two ways of synchronizing in the Java language, the synchronized keyword that can be used in several ways and the volatile keyword that we can use on failed declarations. Those two keywords are related to what is called intrinsic locking. There is also explicit locking and this is what we are going to see first mainly based on the use of a lock interface. Then, we will see that using this lock interface and the condition interface we can implement the wait/notify pattern in a different and more powerful way. And then, we will see what's semaphores are. Semaphores are not a new concept in Java. It is a concept that comes from operating system and that is implemented in other languages. We will see the Java flavor of semaphores.

What Is Wrong with Intrinsic Locking and Synchronization?

Let us introduce intrinsic and explicit locking.

```
public class Person{
        private final Object key =new Object();
        public String init() {
                synchronized(key) {// do some
        stuff}
        }
}
```

If we want to synchronize a method, for instance, here the init method of the Person class. The best way to do that is to create a key object, which can be whatever object, and to place a synchronized block inside this method. This code synchronized of key prevents more than one thread to execute the guarded block of code at the same time. This is called the synchronized pattern in Java and it is well-known. Now what happens if several threads are trying to execute the block of code guarded by the synchronized keyword inside the init method. One of them will be allowed in the block, the others will have to wait for their turn to execute the same block of code. This is the basic synchronization pattern in Java. Now what would happen if a thread is blocked inside the block of code, and when I mean block, I mean probably wrongly blocked. That is, there is some kind of bug in the init method that will prevent a thread from exiting this guarded block of code. Well, it turns out that all the other threads are also blocked. No other thread will be allowed in this block of code. All the threads waiting to enter this block of code are also blocked and there is no way in the JDK nor the JVM to release them. So when this kind of situation occurs, most of the time, the only way to solve this problem is to reboot the JVM, that is to shut down the application, and to load yet again. Of course, this is something that we want to avoid at all costs.

Introducing API Locking with the Lock Interface

The Lock Pattern is precisely here to bring a solution to this case. The Lock Pattern, in fact, brings a richer API to handle exactly this case.
Object key =new Object();
synchronized(key) {// do some stuff}
Instead of writing this code, that is creating a key object and passing this key object to a synchronized block of code, we are going to write this one.

```
Lock lock=new ReentrantLock();
try{
        lock.lock();
        // do some stuff
} finally{
        lock.unlock();
}
```

We create an instance of the Lock interface, the JDK provides an implementing class which is called ReentrantLock, and inside the try finally block of code, we call the lock method of this Lock object and in the finally part call the unlock method, thus guaranteeing that this unlock method will be called when exiting this block of code whatever happens after the lock call. Lock is an interface implemented by a ReentrantLock. It is part of the Java.util.concurrent API introduced in Java 5 in 2004. It offers exactly the same guarantees, that is execution explicitly and read and write ordering, that is visibility, happens before links between operation as the synchronize pattern. And it also provides more functionalities. Why? Because instead of being a language primitive, which is the case for the synchronized block, it is an API, and on this API, we can have many more methods.

Differences Between Synchronization and API Locking

Let us now take a closer look at this pattern. On one hand, we have the synchronized pattern. We create instance of any object to use the monitor defined on this object and this object can be used to guard as many block of code as we need. On this lock pattern, we create a Lock object instance of the Lock interface and the biggest difference is that on this lock object we have the methods of the lock interface and this is through the use of those methods that we will have more patterns and more functionalities for guarding blocks of code and for handling lock acquisition.

Lock Patterns: Interruptible Lock Acquisition

So what does this lock pattern bring to us?
- Interruptible lock acquisition
- Timed lock acquisition
- Fair lock acquisition

First, it brings interruptible lock acquisition. Let us see that on example.

```
Lock lock=new ReentrantLock();
try{
        lock.lock();
        // do some stuff
} finally{
        lock.unlock();
}
```
Here we have the basic pattern with the lock
method call that will guard the block of code
between the lock and the unlock call.
```
Lock lock=new ReentrantLock();
try{
        lock.lockInterruptibly();
        // do some stuff
} finally{
        lock.unlock();
}
```
Instead of that, we can call lockInterruptibly
which will have the same kind of semantic as
the lock call, that is the thread calling this
method will be blocked until the guarded
block of code can be executed. Now if another
thread has a reference of it, it can call the
interrupt method on the thread and the
lockInterruptibly method instead of letting it
execute the code where through itself the
interrupted exception, thus reading the
waiting thread. This was not possible with the
synchronized pattern. This can be costly. It
can be hard to achieve from a pure
implementation prospective, but it is possible.
It is available as a functionality.

Lock Patterns: Timed Lock Acquisition

The second thing we can do is called Timed lock acquisition. What does it mean now?

```
Lock lock=new ReentrantLock();
if (lock.tryLock()) {
        try{
                // guarded block of code
        } finally{
                lock.unlock();
        }
} else { ... }
```

It means that instead of calling the lock method, we can call the tryLock method and this time if a thread is already executing the guarded block of code, the tryLock called will return false immediately. So instead of being block, our thread will not enter the guarded block of code and will be able to do something else immediately.

```
Lock lock=new ReentrantLock();
if (lock.tryLock(1, TimeUnit.SECONDS)) {
        try{
                // guarded block of code
        } finally{
                lock.unlock();
        }
} else { ... }
```

Note that we can also pass a timeout to this tryLock method, for example, here our thread will wait for 1 second. If the guarded block of code is still not available after this timeout, it will execute the else block of code.

Lock Patterns: Fair Lock Acquisition

And the third functionality we have is called fair lock acquisition. How does it work? Suppose we have several threads waiting for a given lock. Whether it is an intrinsic or explicit lock, the first one to enter the guarded block of code is chosen randomly. This is the default behavior of both the synchronized keyword and the Lock object. Fairness means that the first to enter the wait line will also be the first to enter the guarded block of code. Let us see that on an example.

```
Lock lock=new ReentrantLock();
try{
        lock.lock();
        // guarded block of code
} finally{
        lock.unlock();
}
```

By default, a ReentrantLock built in the normal way is non-fair, meaning that if two threads are waiting to acquire this lock, we do not know in advance which one is going to execute the guarded block of code first.

```
Lock lock=new ReentrantLock(true);
try{
        lock.lock();
        // guarded block of code
} finally{
        lock.unlock();
}
```

Now if we pass the true Boolean when building this Lock object, this Lock object becomes a fair ReentrantLock or a fair lock. It means that if two threads are waiting to acquire this lock, the first one to the guarded block of code will be the first that enter the wait list. Achieving this is costly, so using fairness is not activated by default and you should really use that only if you need it absolutely.

Wrapping-up the Lock Pattern

As we can see, using this lock interface gives our code and our applications some wiggle room. A lock can be interrupted. It's possible, it is hard to achieve, but it has been done, and it is indeed costly in our application. But if we definitely need it, then it is available. The acquisition of this Lock object can also be blocked for a certain amount of time. I can ask this Lock object and tell hey if in once again from now the lock is not available, then I prefer to leave and do something else. And at last, this acquisition can be fair letting in the threads on a first come, first serve basis and the same goes as for the interruptible lock. It is a costly functionality to activate, so use it only when you definitely need it.

Producer / Consumer Pattern: Wait / Notify Implementation

Let us see now how we can implement the producer/consumer pattern using this lock interface. The classical way to implement this with the intrinsic locking is probably to use the wait and notify pattern. Wait and notify are methods from the Object class that should be called from inside the synchronized block of code. Obviously, since explicit locking does not work with synchronized block of code, the wait/notify pattern cannot work at all. So we need another pattern and this is what we are going to see now. Let us have a quick look on this classical way of implementing this pattern.

```
Object lock =newObject();
class Producer {
        public void produce() {
                synchronized(lock) {
                        while (isFull(buffer))
                                lock.wait();
                        buffer[count++] = 1;
                        lock.notifyAll();
                }
        }
}
class Consumer{
        public void consume() {
                synchronized(lock) {
                        while(isEmpty(buffer))
                                lock.wait();
                        buffer[--count] = 0;
                        lock.notifyAll();
                }
        }
}
```

Here is the code of the producer and here is the code of the consumer. Those two classes are organized around synchronized block. If the buffer is full, then the producing thread has to wait, and to be awaken, the consumer thread once it has removed an element from the buffer has to call notify or notifyAll on the same block object. This will have the effect of awaking a producing thread that can carry on. And the same goes on the other side. If the buffer is empty, consumer thread cannot, of course, consume any element, so it has to wait, and to be awaken, it has to be notified by a producing thread. One major caveat of this pattern is that one thread is in this wait state. Once it has called this wait method, it is blocked and there is no way we can interrupt it. So if no thread is ever calling notify or notifyAll, there is no chance that this thread will be awakened. The only way to interrupt it will be to reboot the application to reboot the Java machine itself.

Producer / Consumer Pattern: Lock Implementation with Condition

Let us address this problem and others by using this lock pattern.

```
Lock lock =new ReentrantLock();
class Producer {
        public void produce() {
                try{
                        lock.lock();
                        while (isFull(buffer))
                                // wait
                        buffer[count++] = 1;
                        // notify
                } finally{
                        lock.unlock();
                }
        }
}
class Consumer {
```

```
public void consume() {
    try{
        lock.lock();
        while (isEmpty(buffer))
            // wait
        buffer[--count] = 0;
        // notify
    } finally{
        lock.unlock();
    }
}
}
```

Here is the producer. We just translated the synchronized block with this new lock pattern and we have the same organization of the code for the consumer. Now inside this guarded block of code, we still have the same structure. While the buffer is full, we have to put this thread in a wait state, and on the consuming side, when an element is consumed from the buffer, the consumer has to notify the producer that there is room in the buffer. How can this be done?

```
Lock lock=new ReentrantLock();
Condition notFull=lock.newCondition();
Condition notEmpty= lock.newCondition();
class Producer{
    public void produce() {
        try{
            lock.lock();
            while(isFull(buffer))
                notFull.await();
            buffer[count++] = 1;
            notEmpty.signal();
        } finally{
            lock.unlock();
        }
    }
}
```

```
class Consumer{
    public void consume() {
        try{
            lock.lock();
            while(isEmpty(buffer))
                notEmpty.await();
            buffer[--count] = 0;
            notFull.signal();
        } finally{
            lock.unlock();
        }
    }
}
```

Well, it is done with a new object of type
condition and created from this Lock object
by calling the new condition method. The first
condition here is called notFull. We are going
to call notFull.await on the producing side and
notFull.signal on the consuming side. This
await method is the equivalent of the wait
method from the wait/notify pattern and this
signal method is the equivalent of the notify
method. To do it in the other way, we can
create a second condition object, this time
called notEmpty. We are going to call
notEmpty.await if the buffer is empty and if a
consumer wants to consume an object and
notEmpty.signal once a producer has added
an object to the buffer. So here is the full
pattern we have at the end of the day. It looks
like the wait/notify pattern, but does not use
synchronize blocks.

The Condition Object:
Interruptibility and Fairness

This condition object is the new object we
introduce here. It is used to park and to awake
threads in this pattern. It is built from the
Lock object and a Lock object can have any
number of Condition object linked to it. Now
we need to be a little careful because this
condition object as all the Java objects extends
the object class so it has a wait and a notify
method. Those methods should not be taken
for await and signal. In fact, if we try to use
them, they will not work since we are not in a
synchronized block of code. What does this
pattern bring to us? In fact, it brings many
things. The await call is blocking, but, and this
is the difference with the wait call from the
object class, it can be interrupted. We can
interrupt the thread that is blocked on this
await call. It was not the case on the wait
method from the Object class.

- await()
- await(time,timeUnit)
- awaitNanos(nanosTimeout)
- awaitUntil(date)
- awaitUninterruptibly()

In fact, there are five versions of this await
method, the plain await method that we used,
three await methods that takes timeout, that
can be expressed in timeUnits, for instance, 2
seconds, or in nanoseconds, and an awaitUntil
that takes a date as a parameter, a date, of
course, some time in the future. And if we do
not want this await call to be interrupted, we
can also call awaitUninterruptibly. That will

prevent the interruption of a thread to interrupt this method call. So this API give us ways to prevent the blocking of waiting threads with the Condition API. Our last nodes, we saw that it was possible to create fair locks and a fair lock will generate fair conditions. That is, if several threads are calling this await method one at a time, they will be awakened in the same order.

Wrapping-up the Lock and Condition Objects

We can now wrap up this part on lock and condition. Lock and condition is another implementation of the wait/notify pattern. It gives wiggle room to build better concurrent systems by providing a way to control interruptibility, to control timeouts in concurrent locking and lock acquisition, and to give fairness to our systems.

Introducing the ReadWriteLock Pattern

Let us now talk about read/write locks. In some cases, not to say in most of the cases, what we need is exclusive writes. That is what I want to do is to guard the block of code that is going to modify a variable or a collection, for instance, or a map, but I want to allow for parallel reads of this variable or of this collection or map. And this is not how regular locks work. That is, if I guard the block of

53

code that is going to modify this variable and the block of code that is going to read it, I will have exclusive writes and also exclusive reads. This is what the read/write lock does and this is what we are going to see now. A ReadWriteLock is an interface with only two methods. First method is readLock to get a read lock, and the second method, very simple, is writeLock to get a write lock. Both this readLock and this writeLock are instances of lock, the Lock interface that we just saw. Now the rules are the following.
Only one thread can hold the writelock
When the writelock isheld, no one can hold the readlock
As many threads as needed can hold the readlock
Only one thread can hold the writeLock. When the writeLock is held, no one can hold the readLock. And of course, as many threads as needed can hold the readLock. It means that if I guard a block of code with a writeLock, the execution of this block of code would be exclusive. And if I guard another block of code with the readLock, this block of code will be available for as many threads as I need.

Implementing an Efficient Concurrent Cache with ReadWriteLock

Let us see that on an example. ReadWriteLock is an interface and ReentrantReadWriteLock is the implementing class provided by the JDK.

```
ReadWriteLock readWritelock= new
ReentrantReadWriteLock();
Lock readLock= readWritelock.readLock();
Lock writeLock= readWritelock.writeLock();
```

From this readWriteLock object, I create two locks, readLock and writeLock with the readLock and writeLock method. And since I got those two locks from the same readWriteLock, they form a pair of read and write locks. This point is very important. Those two locks can be used to create a thread-safe cache.

```
Map<Long, User> cache= new HashMap<>();
try{
        readLock.lock();
        return cache.get(key);
} finally{
        readLock.unlock();
}
```

A cache can be implemented using a basic HashMap. Here we have a Map of Long and User, which could be a cache to a database, long being the primary key of the user. Reading this cache is guarded by the readLock, by the same pattern as the pattern we saw using a basic Lock object. Knowing the semantic of this readLock object, we know that any number of thread can read this cache at the same time.

```
Map<Long, User> cache= new HashMap<>();
try{
        writeLock.lock();
        cache.put(key,value);
} finally{
        writeLock.unlock();
}
```

Now this is the modification of the map guarded by the writeLock, once again, with the same pattern, but this time this writeLocking protects the modification of the cache and will prevent concurrent read that could read corrupted value. It could also be achieved using a ConcurrentHashMap. We will see that in the fifth and last module of this book.

Wrapping-up the ReadWriteLock Pattern

- Write operations are exclusive of other writes and reads
- Read operations can be made in parallel

Let us do a quick wrap-up on this read/write lock notion. It works on a single ReadWriteLock object that is used to get a write lock and a read lock. It is very important to understand that this pair of read and write locks must be created from the same ReadWriteLock object. The write operations are exclusive of other writes and reads, so when a thread is modifying, for instance, the cache object that we just created, no other threads can modify it and no other thread can read from it, but the read operations are free. They can be made in parallel. So it allows for extremely good throughput, especially if we have many reads and few writes, which is usually the assumption made when we create caches.

Introducing the Semaphore Pattern, First Example

Let us see now the last part of this module about semaphores. Semaphores is a well-known concept in concurrent programming. It does not come from Java. It comes from the very early days of the unique operating systems. It looks like a lock, and in fact, it is some kind of a lock, but instead of allowing only one thread in the guarded block of code, it allows for more than one, and in fact, a semaphore is built and a number of permits and this number of permits is the number of threads allowed in this block of code. Let us see that on an example.

```java
Semaphore semaphore=new Semaphore(5); // permits
try{
        semaphore.acquire();
        // guarded block of code
} finally{
        semaphore.release();
}
```

We have a Semaphore class. When we create a semaphore in Java, we have to fix the number of permits on which the semaphore is built and then there is an acquire method and a release method to acquire a permit and be allowed in a guarded block of code and to release this permit. A semaphore built in the normal way, and the default way, is non-fair. It means that if there are threads waiting for permits, they will be accepted randomly in the guarded block of code. This acquire method, of course, is blocking until a permit is made available. So in our example, only 5 threads would be allowed to execute the guarded block of code at the same time. A semaphore can be made fair.

```
Semaphore semaphore=new
Semaphore(5,true); // fair
try{
        semaphore.acquire(2);
        // guarded block of code
} finally{
        semaphore.release(2);
}
```

If I pass the true Boolean and the second parameter of the construction of this object, each will create a fair semaphore. And I can also ask for more than one permit at a time. Acquire 2 here will ask for 2 permits, and if there is only 1 available, the thread executing this code will have to wait for a second 1 to be released. Of course, if we ask for two permits, we should also release two permits.

Semaphore Pattern: Interruptibility and Timed Permit Acquisition

```
Semaphore semaphore=new Semaphore(5);
try{
        semaphore.acquireUninterruptibly();
        // guarded block of code
} finally{
        semaphore.release();
}
```

This API has been built on the same ideas as the lock API, so I can also handle interruptibility and timeouts on the semaphore API. If I call the interrupt method on a thread that is blocked on an acquire call, this thread will throw an InterruptedException at once. If I do not want this behavior, then I can call the acquireUninterruptibly method on this semaphore object, and in this case, this thread cannot be interrupted. The only way to free aim is by calling its release method. Now if I interrupt this thread, it will not do anything at the moment of this method call. But if a permit becomes available, this thread will not be allowed in the guarded block of code. It will instead throw this InterruptedException. Once again, following the same ideas as the lock interface, acquisition can be made immediate.

```
Semaphore semaphore=new Semaphore(5);
try{
        if(semaphore.tryAcquire())
                // guarded block of code
        else
                // I could not enter the guarded
        code
} finally{
        semaphore.release();
}
```

TryAcquire will see if a permit is available, and if it is not the case, it will fail, written false, and I will be able to execute some other code than the guarded block of code. I can also pass a timeout to this tryAcquire method call so that this method will have written false after this timeout.

```
Semaphore semaphore=new Semaphore(5);
try{
        if(semaphore.tryAcquire(1,
        TimeUnit.SECONDS))
                // guarded block of code
```

```
else
        // I could not enter the guarded
    code
} finally{
    semaphore.release();
}
```

Wrapping-up the Semaphore Pattern, Control of the Waiting Threads

We just saw the pattern, how to use a semaphore object, but it is not all. We also have specific methods on this Semaphore object that do not exist on a classical Lock object. Those methods make a semaphore more than just a lock with more than one permit. In fact, we have methods to handle both the permits and the waiting threads. First, we can reduce the number of permits after the semaphore has been created. It is not possible to increase this number of permits. We also have method to check if there are waiting threads on this semaphore. Are there any waiting thread? How many threads are waiting? And we can also get the collection of the waiting thread, which is not possible on the Lock object. So we can now quickly wrap up this part on the Semaphore object. The Semaphore is built on the number of permits. Those permits can be acquired in different ways and must be released by the threads. This part of the API is basically the same as the Lock API, the only difference being that a lock has only one permit and a semaphore has more than one. But beside that, it is also possible to query a semaphore for the number of waiting threads. Are there any waiting threads? How many? And we can also get references on the threads.

Java Coding: Producer / Consumer Based on the Lock Pattern

Okay, time to see some code in action. What are we going to see in this Java coding session? Well, we are going to see this producer/consumer pattern using the lock interface and this Condition object. We will also see how a read/write lock can be set to create a concurrent cache. Let us see this producer/consumer pattern in action using the lock interface.

```
package executors;
import java.util.ArrayList;
import java.util.List;
import java.util.concurrent.Callable;
import java.util.concurrent.locks.Lock;
import java.util.concurrent.locks.ReentrantLock;
public class ProcucerConsumerWithLocks {
    public static void main(String[] args)
throws InterruptedException {
        List<Integer> buffer = new
ArrayList<>();
        Lock lock = new ReentrantLock();
        class Consumer implements
Callable<String> {
            public String call() throws
InterruptedException {
                int count = 0;
```

```java
                    while (count++ < 50) {
                        try {
                            lock.lock();
                            while
(isEmpty(buffer))
                                // wait
                                buffer.remov
e(buffer.size() - 1);
                                // signal
                        } finally {
                            lock.unlock();
                        }
                    }
                    return "Consumed " +
(count - 1);
            }
        }
        class Producer implements
Callable<String> {
            public String call() throws
InterruptedException {
                int count = 0;
                while (count++ < 50) {
                    try {
                        lock.lock();
                        while
(isFull(buffer))
                            // wait
                            buffer.add(1)
;
                            // signal
                    } finally {
                        lock.unlock();
                    }
                }
                return "Produced " +
(count - 1);
            }
        }
```

```
    }
    public static boolean
isEmpty(List<Integer> buffer) {
        return buffer.size() == 0;
    }
    public static boolean isFull(List<Integer>
buffer) {
        return buffer.size() == 10;
    }
}
```

So we have a shared buffer that is just a List
of Integers. And then Lock object of type lock,
the interface provided by the JDK and
implemented by ReentrantLock, which is the
standard implementation of lock interface,
also available in the JDK. Then we have this
Consumer class implementation of the
Callable of String interface. It has a single
method call that return a string of character
and it is going to try to consume 50 elements
from that buffer by just removing elements
from the end of the buffer. And block of code
is guarded by Lock object, lock.lock and
lock.unlock. And once all of the items have
been consumed, we just return the message
that we Consumed the right number of items.
Now we needed to add some code here in
order to guarantee that lock.unlock method
call will be called whatever happens between
the locking of the subject and the last
instruction of the block. Suppose for instance,
the method throws an exception or something
wrong happens, if this lock.unlock is not
called, then lock will not be released and we
will have a dead lock in our application. To
ensure that, there is one very simple way, is to
put block of code in a try block and to add the
finally close and put our unlock call in it.
Thus, if something wrong happens in the

block of code, before leaving the method, we have the guarantee of the language level that unlock method will be called. Let us now take a look at the producer. The producer is basically the same. It also has a lock and unlock call. We wait while the buffer isFull, and once there is room in it, we'll add an element to the buffer. Once again, we need to make sure that unlock is called. So let us add a finally close for our code to be correct.

Java Coding: Setting up Conditions on the Producer / Consumer

```
package executors;
import java.util.ArrayList;
import java.util.List;
import java.util.concurrent.Callable;
import
java.util.concurrent.ExecutionException;
import java.util.concurrent.ExecutorService;
import java.util.concurrent.Executors;
import java.util.concurrent.Future;
import java.util.concurrent.locks.Condition;
import java.util.concurrent.locks.Lock;
import
java.util.concurrent.locks.ReentrantLock;
public class ProcucerConsumerWithLocks {
    public static void main(String[] args)
throws InterruptedException {
        List<Integer> buffer = new
ArrayList<>();
        Lock lock = new ReentrantLock();
        Condition isEmpty =
lock.newCondition();
```

```java
        Condition isFull =
lock.newCondition();
        class Consumer implements
Callable<String> {
            public String call() throws
InterruptedException {
                int count = 0;
                while (count++ < 50) {
                    try {
                        lock.lock();
                        while
(isEmpty(buffer)) {
                            // wait
                            isEmpty.awai
t();
                        }
                        buffer.remove(buf
fer.size() - 1);
                        // signal
                        isFull.signalAll();
                    } finally {
                        lock.unlock();
                    }
                }
                return "Consumed " +
(count - 1);
            }
        }
        class Producer implements
Callable<String> {
            public String call() throws
InterruptedException {
                int count = 0;
                while (count++ < 50) {
                    try {
                        lock.lock();
                        while
(isFull(buffer)) {
                            // wait
```

65

```
                                isFull.await()
;
                          }
                          buffer.add(1);
                          // signal
                          isEmpty.signalAll(
);
                    } finally {
                          lock.unlock();
                    }
                }
                return "Produced " +
(count - 1);
            }
        }
        List<Producer> producers = new
ArrayList<>();
        for (int i = 0; i < 4; i++) {
            producers.add(new Producer());
        }
        List<Consumer> consumers = new
ArrayList<>();
        for (int i = 0; i < 4; i++) {
            consumers.add(new
Consumer());
        }

        System.out.println("Producers and
Consumers launched");

        List<Callable<String>>
producersAndConsumers = new
ArrayList<>();
        producersAndConsumers.addAll(pr
oducers);
        producersAndConsumers.addAll(co
nsumers);
        ExecutorService executorService =
Executors.newFixedThreadPool(8);
```

```
        try {
                List<Future<String>> futures =
executorService.invokeAll(producersAndCons
umers);
                futures.forEach(
                        future -> {
                                try {
                                        System.out.p
rintln(future.get());
                                } catch
(InterruptedException | ExecutionException
e) {
                                        System.out.p
rintln("Exception: " + e.getMessage());
                                }
                        });
        } finally {
                executorService.shutdown();
                System.out.println("Executor
service shut down");
        }
    }
    public static boolean
isEmpty(List<Integer> buffer) {
        return buffer.size() == 0;
    }
    public static boolean isFull(List<Integer>
buffer) {
        return buffer.size() == 10;
    }
}
```

Output at console :
Producers and Consumers launched
Produced 50
Produced 50
Produced 50
Produced 50
Consumed 50
Consumed 50

Consumed 50
Consumed 50
Executor service shut down
Now we need to add some code here in the
case the buffer isEmpty and we cannot
consume any element from it. The code we
need to add here works with a Condition
object built on Lock object. Let us create
condition object. Condition. We are going to
call this condition isEmpty and it is simply
built by calling the newCondition method on
this Lock object. Let us take this isEmpty
object and call Empty.await. It will have the
effect of parking thread and releasing the lock
from Lock object, and to unpark thread, we
need to signal it from the producer once the
producer has added an element to the buffer.
So here, isEmpty will be signaled to unpark
the consumer thread, and we need to do the
same kind of thing on the producer part. Once
a producer has produced, if the buffer is full,
the producer cannot produce any element
here, so we need to park the producing thread
with another condition. Let us create other
condition that will be called isFull created in
the exact same way newCondition. This isFull
condition will be used to park the producing
thread if the buffer is full, and once the
consumer has consumed an element here, we
will signal the producing thread that it can
continue to run. So we have our Consumer
and Producer class working. Let us take a
look at the rest of the code. First, we create a
list of 4 producers and a list of 4 consumers
then we are going to add them all to
producersAndConsumers List of Callable,
create an ExecutorService with the right
number of threads. We have four producers
and four consumers, so we are going to add

eight threads to this ExecutorService and invoke all those callables in the ExecutorService with this invokeAll method from the ExecutorService that takes a collection of callable as a parameter. It will return the List of Futures, and for each of those futures, we are going to execute this code here. Basically, we are just going to print out the message returned by the producer and the consumer. This get method may throw an InterruptedException or ExecutionException, so we just print out the message if this is the case. And once again, since we are using an ExecutorService here, we shut it down in a finally close of a try block. So let us run this code now. We can see that our 4 producers have been producing 50 elements each and have been consumed by the all the consumers and the ExecutorService has been properly shut down.

Java Coding: Setting up the Right Number of Threads

Let us see now what happens if the ExecutorService is not set to the right number of threads.
ExecutorService executorService = Executors.newFixedThreadPool(4);
Suppose we put only four threads in it, let us run the previous code, and what we can see is that nothing happens. Obviously, our system is blocked. It is still running because we can see the Java virtual machine is still running, but it seems to be blocked. Let us stop it and let us run it again, but this time in debug

mode. We can now switch to the debug prospect here. Here we have all the threads of our application, the main thread, which is handling everything and the four threads of our ExecutorService. Let us pose one and see where it is.

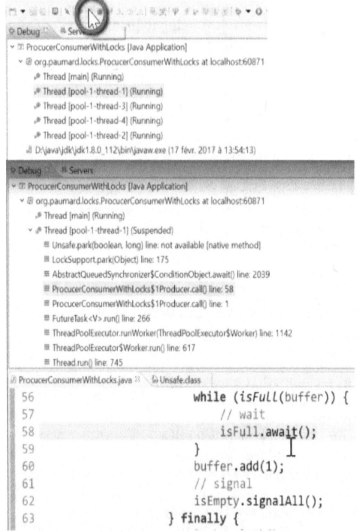

We can see that it is blocked on the Line 58 of our code, which is this await method. What is happening in fact this await call releases the lock of this object, but does not release the producing thread. It means that this thread is parked is still executing our task and cannot take another task, for instance, the consumer. Since we have only four threads, what happened is that those four threads are running our four producers and there is no thread available to run our consumers. So basically, our producers have filled the buffer waiting for some room to be made a consumer, but no consumer has any chance to be executed since there is no thread available. So when you design this kind of system, just be aware that this is the total number of threads available, and if you are in a consumer/producer pattern, you need to make sure that you have enough threads to run all your consumers and your producers. The only solution here is to kill the JVM by clicking red button.

Java Coding: Dealing with Exceptions with Timeouts

Let us now suppose that there is a problem in our producer and for some reason it is not going to produce any data.

```java
class Producer implements Callable<String> {
   public String call() throws
InterruptedException {
     int count = 0;
     while (count++ < 50) {
       try {
           lock.lock();
          int i = 10 / 0;
          while (isFull(buffer)) {
              // wait
```

```
        isFull.await();
    }
```
// rest of the codes are same
Let us simulate an exception here, for
instance, a division by 0 exception, and let us
run this code. What we can see is that once
again our system seems to be locked. The JVM
is still running, but nothing is happening. In
fact, we can analyze this problem quite easily.
The exception is thrown here. Since we are in
a try finally block, this code will be executed,
so this producer will release the thread it is in,
and once this is done, no production of an
element will ever occur. So what happens on
the consuming side? Well, our four consumers
will be calling this await method, but since no
producer will ever call this signalAll method,
the consuming threads will never be unparked
from this await call and this is then just locked
down. So how can we work around this fact?
Well, as we saw in the previously, it is possible
to add a timeout to this await method.

```
class Consumer implements Callable<String>
{
public String call() throws
InterruptedException {
    int count = 0;
    while (count++ < 50) {
        try {
        lock.lock();
        while (isEmpty(buffer)) {
        // wait
        isEmpty.await(10,
TimeUnit.MILLISECONDS);
        }
```

This version of the await method returns void
meaning that it does not return anything in
fact, of course. If we add a timeout to it,
suppose then MILLISECONDS. Alright, what

does it mean? It means that if after 10 ms nothing happened, it's probably that there is something wrong on the producing side, so of course, this timeout has to be tuned for your application and for your needs. Here 10 ms is enough, and this time, this await method returns a Boolean. So after 10 ms, this await call will return. It will not block forever and it will return with a false value.

Java Coding: Setting up Timeout to Unlock a Producer / Consumer

```java
package executors;
import java.util.ArrayList;
import java.util.List;
import java.util.concurrent.Callable;
import java.util.concurrent.ExecutionException;
import java.util.concurrent.ExecutorService;
import java.util.concurrent.Executors;
import java.util.concurrent.Future;
import java.util.concurrent.TimeUnit;
import java.util.concurrent.TimeoutException;
import java.util.concurrent.locks.Condition;
import java.util.concurrent.locks.Lock;
import java.util.concurrent.locks.ReentrantLock;
public class ProcucerConsumerWithLocks {
    public static void main(String[] args) throws InterruptedException {
        List<Integer> buffer = new ArrayList<>();
        Lock lock = new ReentrantLock();
```

```java
        Condition isEmpty =
lock.newCondition();
        Condition isFull =
lock.newCondition();
        class Consumer implements
Callable<String> {
            public String call() throws
InterruptedException, TimeoutException {
                int count = 0;
                while (count++ < 50) {
                    try {
                        lock.lock();
                        while
(isEmpty(buffer)) {
                            // wait
                            if
(!isEmpty.await(10,
TimeUnit.MILLISECONDS)) {
                                throw
new TimeoutException("Consumer time
out");
                            }
                        }
                        buffer.remove(buf
fer.size() - 1);
                        // signal
                        isFull.signalAll();
                    } finally {
                        lock.unlock();
                    }
                }
                return "Consumed " +
(count - 1);
            }
        }
        class Producer implements
Callable<String> {
            public String call() throws
InterruptedException {
```

```java
                    int count = 0;
                    while (count++ < 50) {
                        try {
                            lock.lock();
                            int i = 10 / 0;
                            while
(isFull(buffer)) {

                                // wait
                                isFull.await()
;

                            }
                            buffer.add(1);
                            // signal
                            isEmpty.signalAll(
);

                        } finally {
                            lock.unlock();
                        }
                    }
                    return "Produced " +
(count - 1);
                }
            }
        List<Producer> producers = new
ArrayList<>();
            for (int i = 0; i < 4; i++) {
                producers.add(new Producer());
            }
        List<Consumer> consumers = new
ArrayList<>();
            for (int i = 0; i < 4; i++) {
                consumers.add(new
Consumer());
            }
        System.out.println("Producers and
Consumers launched");
        List<Callable<String>>
producersAndConsumers = new
ArrayList<>();
```

```java
        producersAndConsumers.addAll(pr
oducers);
        producersAndConsumers.addAll(co
nsumers);
        ExecutorService executorService =
Executors.newFixedThreadPool(8);
        try {
            List<Future<String>> futures =
executorService.invokeAll(producersAndCons
umers);
                futures.forEach(future -> {
                    try {
                        System.out.println(fut
ure.get());
                    } catch
(InterruptedException | ExecutionException
e) {
                        System.out.println("E
xception: " + e.getMessage());
                    }
                });
        } finally {
            executorService.shutdown();
            System.out.println("Executor
service shut down");
        }
    }
    public static boolean
isEmpty(List<Integer> buffer) {
        return buffer.size() == 0;
    }
    public static boolean isFull(List<Integer>
buffer) {
        return buffer.size() == 10;
    }
}
```
Output at console ;
Producers and Consumers launched

Exception: java.lang.ArithmeticException: / by zero
Exception: java.lang.ArithmeticException: / by zero
Exception: java.lang.ArithmeticException: / by zero
Exception: java.lang.ArithmeticException: / by zero
Exception: java.util.concurrent.TimeoutException: Consumer time out
Exception: java.util.concurrent.TimeoutException: Consumer time out
Exception: java.util.concurrent.TimeoutException: Consumer time out
Exception: java.util.concurrent.TimeoutException: Consumer time out
Executor service shut down

So what we can do is the following, wrap this in an if call and if we get the false value for this call, then we can throw, for instance, a new timeout exception with the message Consumer time out, okay, and add this TimeoutException here to the call method of our callable. Now our producer will still fail to produce any elements in the buffer, but after 10 ms, our consumer will stop waiting for nothing basically and throw this exception. So let us see what it gives them on the executing side. We can see that our 4 producers are throwing this ArithmeticException division by 0 and our 4 consumers are stopping their execution with this TimeoutException here, and of course, no data has been produced and no data has been consumed. So this await method that takes a timeout is a very good way to handle errors in a producer/consumer pattern, and in other patterns, it can be used and should be used to avoid deadlock condition. This was not possible with the wait and notify pattern to implement the producer/consumer.

Java Coding: Creating a Cache with a Race Condition on HashMap

Now let us see how we can use ReadWriteLock to create thread safe and efficient caches. We all know that the HashMap class from the JDK is not thread safe. We can see that on an example. Let us create a very simple, very basic cache, which could be any primary key and string, which could be any value.

```java
package executors;
import java.util.HashMap;
import java.util.Map;
import java.util.Random;
import java.util.concurrent.Callable;
import java.util.concurrent.ExecutorService;
import java.util.concurrent.Executors;
public class CacheWithReadWriteLock {
    private Map<Long, String> cache = new HashMap<>();
    public String put(Long key, String value)
{
        return cache.put(key, value);
    }
    public String get(Long key) {
        return cache.get(key);
    }
```

```java
public static void main(String[] args) {
    CacheWithReadWriteLock cache =
new CacheWithReadWriteLock();
    class Producer implements
Callable<String> {
        private Random rand = new
Random();
        public String call() throws
Exception {
            while (true) {
                long key =
rand.nextInt(1_000);
                cache.put(key,
Long.toString(key));
                if (cache.get(key) ==
null) {
                    System.out.printl
n("Key " + key + " has not been put in the
map");
                }
            }
        }
    }
    ExecutorService executorService =
Executors.newFixedThreadPool(4);
    try {
        for (int i = 0; i < 4; i++) {
            executorService.submit(ne
w Producer());
        }
    } finally {
        executorService.shutdown();
    }
}
}
```
Output at console :
Key 112 has not been put in the map
Key 709 has not been put in the map
Key 95 has not been put in the map

Key 529 has not been put in the map
Key 731 has not been put in the map
Key 818 has not been put in the map
We have two very simple methods on this cache, the put method and a get method. Now let us create a producer that will add forever random key value pairs in this cache. Here, our key value pairs are just numbers and the string value, and just after adding a key value pair, we are going to check if this key is indeed in the cache. There is no remove method in this class, so we do not expect a put to fail. But since we are launching 4 producers in an ExecutorService of size 4, we will have concurrency and things can go wrong. Let us see that by running this code. Indeed, if we run this code, we can see that several keys have not been added to the map due to race conditions in the HashMap class itself. Now the first solution that might come to mind, would be to use the Collections factory class from the JDK, and in that class, the synchronizedMap method, that returns indeed a map that is synchronized. Let us quickly check the implementation of this map. It is an instance of private static member class called SynchronizedMap, and if we check its method, we can see that, in fact, they are all synchronized wrappers on the method from HashMap. So indeed, this solution would work from a pure functional point of view, but it would be extremely inefficient allowing for minimal throughputs on our cache. So we do not want to use this solution. We want to use, of course, a better one.

Java Coding: Fixing the HashMap Cache with ReadWriteLock

So let us go back to our Cache class and create ReadWriteLock.

```java
package executors;
import java.util.HashMap;
import java.util.Map;
import java.util.Random;
import java.util.concurrent.Callable;
import java.util.concurrent.ExecutorService;
import java.util.concurrent.Executors;
import java.util.concurrent.locks.Lock;
import java.util.concurrent.locks.ReadWriteLock;
import java.util.concurrent.locks.ReentrantReadWriteLock;
public class CacheWithReadWriteLock {
    private Map<Long, String> cache = new HashMap<>();
    private ReadWriteLock lock = new ReentrantReadWriteLock();
    private Lock readLock = lock.readLock();
    private Lock writeLock = lock.writeLock();
    public String put(Long key, String value) {
        writeLock.lock();
        try {
            return cache.put(key, value);
        } finally {
            writeLock.unlock();
        }
    }
```

```java
    public String get(Long key) {
        readLock.lock();
        try {
            return cache.get(key);
        } finally {
            readLock.unlock();
        }
    }
    public static void main(String[] args) {
        CacheWithReadWriteLock cache =
new CacheWithReadWriteLock();
        class Producer implements
Callable<String> {
            private Random rand = new
Random();
            public String call() throws
Exception {
                while (true) {
                    long key =
rand.nextInt(1_000);
                    cache.put(key,
Long.toString(key));
                    if (cache.get(key) ==
null) {
                        System.out.printl
n("Key " + key + " has not been put in the
map");
                    }
                }
            }
        }
        ExecutorService executorService =
Executors.newFixedThreadPool(4);
        System.out.println("Adding
value...");
        try {
            for (int i = 0; i < 4; i++) {
                executorService.submit(ne
w Producer());
```

```
            }
        } finally {
            executorService.shutdown();
        }
    }
}
```

Output at console :

Adding value...

The implementation provided by the JDK is called ReentrantReadWriteLock, this one, and from this ReadWriteLock, we can create the first lock that we're going to call readLock = lock.readLock and a second lock that we're going to call writeLock by coding the writeLock method. And with those two locks that are bound together by this ReadWriteLock object, we can create a very efficient cache. This is the put method, so here we want to lock this code using the writeLock, but of course, we are going to put this in a try close because we want to make sure that the writeLock.unlock will be called when we return, and this block of code will ensure that. And we're going to do the same with the read operation on this cache called the readLock method .lock. Put this in a try close, and finally, execute the readLock.unlock method. The way this ReadWriteLock pair works is the following. All the read operations are free and can be made in parallel, so if we have many reads, they will not be blocked. It was not the case on the synchronized version of the collections.SynchronizedMap. The write operation are exclusive. Only one thread can modify the map at the same time, and when a thread is modifying the map, no one can read it. So let us run our code once again with this message to see that we are going to add values to the map, and this time, we can see that no value has been lost. Why? Because all the threads will add the values one by one and one at a time, no more risk condition will occur on the internal structure of this HashMap.

Java Coding Wrap-up

- How to properly lock a Producer / Consumer with Lock
- How to deal with exceptions and timeout
- How HashMapcan fail in a concurrent application
- How to properly synchronize it using a pair of read / write locks

So let us quickly wrap up this Java coding session. What did we see in the code? First of all, we saw how to properly lock the producer/consumer pattern with instances of this lock interface, which is ReentrantLock. We then saw how it was possible to deal with exceptions properly and timeouts using this pattern, which was not possible with the object.wait and notify pattern. And in a second example, we saw the HashMap in action in a concurrent environment and how easy it is to make it fail in such an environment. The HashMap implementation is not thread-safe, so do not use it in a concurrent application without precautions. So we also saw how to properly synchronize it, and for that, we used a pair of read/write locks. We did that to ensure a better throughput, especially with parallel read operations on this map and handle than the fully-synchronized version of the HashMap you can build using the collections.SynchronizeMap method. Last note on this point, we will also see thread-safe implementations of maps, concurrent skip list maps, and concurrent HashMaps in the last module of this book.

Module Wrap-up

- The difference between intrinsic and explicit locking
- Give wiggle room to create efficient concurrent applications
- Locks, read / write locks
- Semaphores
- Interruptibility, timeouts, fairness

Time to wrap up this second module. What did we learn in this second module? Well, we saw the differences between intrinsic and explicit locking, that is locking using APIs. I would say that the most important difference is that explicit locking gives wiggle room to create efficient concurrent applications. From a pure technical point of view, we saw locks and conditions, read/write locks, we saw semaphores, but most important, we saw that those structures allows for interruptibility, timeouts, and fairness, and this is what we call wiggle room here. The next module is about latches and barriers, and we are going to see how to compute things in parallel leveraging those APIs.

Module 3: Controlling Concurrent Applications Using Barriers and Latches

Introduction, Module Agenda

Let us quickly browse through the agenda of this module.

- Two more concurrent primitives :
  - Barrier: to have several tasks waitfor each other
  - Latch: to count down operations and let a task start

What we are going to see is, in fact, two more concurrent primitives. In the previous module, we saw locks, ReadWriteLocks, and semaphores. Here, we are going to see the barrier and the latch. The barrier is there to have several tasks wait for each other, then trigger a subsequent task or action, and then reset the system so that it can run again. This barrier is called a CyclicBarrier for this reason. The latch works almost in the same way, the main difference being that it does not reset. Once a latch has been opened, it cannot be closed again.

Sharing a Task Among Threads and Merging the Results

Let us begin by talking about barriers. Suppose we need to compute something that is a heavy computation and we want to share this computation among several threads. This is a very classical use case. What we could do is divide our data set among several threads. Each thread is given a subtask and what we expect is that each thread will be executed on a given call of our CPU. When all the threads are done, what we need to do is to gather all the results of the computations and merge them, so we need some subsequent task to be triggered to do this merging operation. Let us take a very classical example finding the prime numbers up to a certain value. Here we have 192 numbers to check. You can believe me on this point. Here are the corresponding prime numbers. If we launch this task in the classical way, only one thread will be working and only one core of our CPU will be doing this computation. Of course, we have more one core on our CPU nowaday. On a core I5 or core I7, there are 4 physical cores and 4 more logical cores, so we should be able to go much faster than that.

The Problem of Synchronizing on the End of Tasks

How can we do that? Well, we can divide this (finding prime number) data set into four groups and send each group on one core of our CPU. So the first core will find the prime numbers on its own group, then the second one, then the third one, and then the fourth one. Now there is very little chance that all those cores will end their computations at exactly the same time. The computation they have to do is not exactly the same. They will probably be interrupted by the operating system to contact other tasks, so they will not end at the same time. But once they've all done their computation, what we need to do is to gather all the partial results and add them to the result list to compute the final result of this computation. So once everything is done, we need to trigger this kind of callback task to end the computation. So what do we need from this API? First of all, we need a way to distribute the computation on several threads and we need to know when all the threads have finished their task so that we can launch a callback, a post-processing task, at that moment.

Creating Callable Tasks and Setting up a Barrier

Let us see how the code can be returned. First, we need a task that will take a set of numbers and return the set of prime numbers that this task has found in this set of numbers.
Callable<List<Integer>> task = () -> findPrimes(inputSet);
This task can be implemented using a callable, an interface that we already saw in the first

module of this book. And we are going to use another object that is called the CyclicBarrier. CyclicBarrier barrier = new CyclicBarrier(4); The callable we just wrote is going to be launched several times with different input sets and each callable will be launched in its own thread in parallel. Now, we need to know when all the tasks are done, and for that, we are going to use this CyclicBarrier object. The parameter passed down to the construction of this subject is the number of tasks that will be launched and that the barrier will control. This CyclicBarrier type is, in fact, a concrete class of the java.util.concurrent package, part of the java.util.concurrent API.

Understanding the CyclicBarrier Pattern

Let us see the full pattern of this task.

```
Callable<List<Integer>> task= () -> {
        Set<Integer> result =
        findPrimes(inputSet);
        try{
                barrier.await();// Blocks until
        everybody is ready
        } catch(Exception e) {...}
        return result;
}
```

So we are going to call this findPrimes method that is going to extract the prime numbers from the input set, and once this is done, one, the result has been computed, we will call this barrier.await method, and this await method is going to block until everybody is ready, that is all the callables we just returned are done

89

with their computation. This is the pattern we can use to tell the callable to wait for the barrier to open. In fact, this await call blocks until four calls have been made on it in different threads, four being the number we passed as a parameter when we built this barrier. So how does it work precisely? We have four callables created in the main thread and a barrier object. All these callables are passed to the executor.submit method that we saw in the Executor pattern. They are going to be executed in the ExecutorService and the barrier for the moment is closed, which is its default state when it is created. All those tasks are going to compute the dataset and we all call the await method on this barrier object. Now this barrier object is going to count how many times this await method has been called and when this number of call matches the number on which this barrier has been created, it will open and let the threads continue their execution. After that, we can set up a callback task that will be triggered when the barrier is opened.

Setting up the Full CyclicBarrier Pattern and Launching Tasks

Let us take a closer look at the code. We are going to create a Worker class that implements Callable of List of Integer.
public classWorker implements
Callable<List<Integer>>{
        private CyclicBarrier barrier;
        private List<Integer> inputList;

90

```java
public void Worker(CyclicBarrier
barrier, List<Integer>inputList) {
        this.barrier= barrier;
        this.inputList= inputList;
}
public List<Integer>call() {
        List<Integer>result=
        findPrimes(inputList);
        try{
                barrier.await();
        } catch(InterruptedException|
        BrokenBarrierException e){
                // Error handling
        }
        return result;
    }
}
```

Inside this class, we have two fields, first the inputList in which this worker is supposed to find prime numbers and the barrier that we just talked about. And the call method of the callable interface find the prime numbers among the inputList and then call the await method of the barrier. This is the code of the main thread.

```java
CyclicBarrier barrier= new CyclicBarrier(4);
ExecutorService service=
Executors.newFixedThreadPool(4);
Worker worker1 = new Worker(barrier,
inputList1);
// More workers
Future<List<Integer>> future1 =
service.submit(worker1);
// More submissions
List<Integer> finalResult= new
ArrayList<>(future1.get());
finalResult.addAll(future2.get());
// More results
```

First, we create a CyclicBarrier on four tasks. Of course, we need an ExecutorService with a right number of threads. We create as many workers as we need, probably four workers since we have a barrier and four tasks. We submit the workers one by one to this ExecutorService, get a future, and then get the results from the different future and gather them in the final result.

Waiting for the Barrier with a Time out, Dealing with Exception

We just saw that this await call is a blocking call. Now this barrier API has been designed in the same philosophy as the previous APIs we saw in the previous module, mainly the lock and the semaphore.

- await()
- await(time, timeUnit)

And in fact, we have two versions of this await method, one that is blocking indefinitely and one that can take a timeout, suppose it once again that will be block for once again and then return exceptionally with an InterruptedException in case the barrier did not open. Once opened, a barrier is normally reset, that is it will open, let the thread go through, and then close again. There is a reset method on the barrier so we can call reset manually on the barrier. It will open the barrier, but open it exceptionally. So all the waiting thread, all the waiting tasks on this barrier are going to throw a BrokenBarrierException in that case. There are other cases where this

BrokenBarrierException may be thrown. It can be thrown if a thread is interrupted while waiting on the barrier, so interrupting a thread that is waiting on a given barrier will cause the other thread to throw this BrokenBarrierException, and if the barrier is reset manually, as we just saw, while some threads are waiting for it to open.

Wrapping-up the CyclicBarrier

Let us now quickly wrap up what we saw on this CyclicBarrier. A CyclicBarrier is a tool that we can use to synchronize several threads between them and let them continue with their work when they have reached a common point. A CyclicBarrier is closed when created and will open when all the threads have reached this common point, and then will close again allowing for cyclic computations. It can also be reset manually, but in this case, the waiting threads on this barrier will throw a BrokenBarrierException. And at last, it is also possible to set timeouts on the threads that are waiting for a barrier to open. So if something goes wrong in our computation, the system is not blocked, the threads can still be freed with, of course, an InterruptedException.

Introducing the Latch, a Barrier That Cannot Be Reset

Let us now talk about latches. Latches are objects that closely look like barriers, but it is not the same, and we are going to see the differences between them. Let us examine a new use case. We need to start our application and this application is a quite complex one. It depends on many services, suppose AuthenticationService, DataService to access the database, OrderService to handle orders from our customers, probably many more. And of course, we need to make sure that all those services have properties started before we start our main application. So before serving clients, our application needs to make sure that all those resources are properly initialized. It looks like it is a problem for the CyclicBarrier. The problem is that once all the services are available, once they have all properties started, we need to start our application, but we do not want the barrier to reset. We do not want the barrier to close again because it could block everything, the system will have impression that some services have not been properly started. So it is the fact that this barrier is cycling that we cannot use this object in this case. What we need, in fact, is a kind of barrier that once opened cannot be closed again and this is exactly the job for this new object called the countdownlatch that we are going to see now.

Understanding the CountDownLatch Pattern

The countdownLatch works almost the same as a CyclicBarrier. Suppose we have three tasks in callable in the main thread and a Latch object we are going to see how to create one in the next page. We pass everything to the ExecutorService and our tasks are going to execute. At some point, all our tasks will be waiting on the latch and this will have the same effect as the barrier. It will open the latch and let the task continue their execution. But the big difference is that the latch does not reset. It does not close again.

A CountDownLatch in Action to Start an Application

How this is going to work in the code. Well, we can create a ServiceWorker.

```
public class ServiceWorker implements
Callable<List<Integer>>{
        private CountDownLatch latch;
        private Service service;
        public
        booleanWorker(CountDownLatchlatch
        , Service service) {
                this.latch= latch;
                this.service= service;
        }
        public void call() {
                service.init();
                latch.countDown();
        }
}
```

The task of this worker is to launch a given service, think about the AuthenticationService and the like. It implements callable. When I create such a worker, I pass a given latch to it and the service I want to start and this call method implementation of the callable interface does two things. First, it calls the init

95

method of that service that will properly initialize this service. This can take some time, especially if I have network access and the like. And once this is done, I am going to call the countdown method on this Latch object. On the main thread side, I create this CountDownLatch object with three services to launch.

```
CountDownLatch latch= new
CountDownLatch(3);
ExecutorService
executor=Executors.newFixedThreadPool(4);
ServiceWorker worker1= new
ServiceWorker(latch,dataService);
// More workers
Future<Boolean> future1=
executor.submit(worker1);
// More submissions
try{
        latch.await(10, TimeUnit.SECONDS);
        // blocks until the //count reaches 0
        server.start();
} catch(InterruptedExceptione){
        // Error handling
}
```

This CountDownLatch class is a class from the Java.util.Concurrent package and then ExecutorService with four threads in it. Then I can create as many workers as I need to initialize my services. Here, I suppose that I have three services. I will submit those workers in my Executor. This Executor will execute them and then all I have to do is wait for this latch to open by calling its await method. This await method will block until the count of the latch reaches 0, and when this is the case, I can call my server.start method that will start my overall server and that will trigger the servicing of my customers. Now here I have used the await with the timeout method. It will block for only 10 seconds, which is I guess enough time to start my application.

Wrapping-up the CountDownLatch Pattern

So we can now wrap up this simple object CountDownLatch. This latch is just a tool to check that different threads did their task properly. Once this is the case, we can synchronize the beginning of subsequent tasks on the last one to complete. The difference with the CyclicBarrier is that once open, the CountDownLatch cannot be closed again, so it makes it a very good tool to control the firing up of an application.

Java Coding: A CyclicBarrier with a Callback Task in Action

we are going to see a full example with a CyclicBarrier in action, several threads that are going to do some stuff, trigger this barrier, open this barrier, and trigger a call by corporation on it. Let us see now CyclicBarriers in action. Suppose we have four friends who decided to go to the cinema together and they also want to queue together, but of course, they live in different places in the city, so they decide to meet at a nearby cafe and then to go to the cinema together. So friend is modeled by a Callable.

```java
package executors;
import java.util.ArrayList;
import java.util.List;
import java.util.Random;
import java.util.concurrent.Callable;
import java.util.concurrent.CyclicBarrier;
import
java.util.concurrent.ExecutionException;
import java.util.concurrent.ExecutorService;
import java.util.concurrent.Executors;
import java.util.concurrent.Future;
import java.util.concurrent.TimeUnit;
import
java.util.concurrent.TimeoutException;
public class BarrierInAction {
    public static void main(String[] args) {
        class Friend implements
Callable<String> {
                private CyclicBarrier barrier;
                public Friend(CyclicBarrier
barrier) {
                    this.barrier = barrier;
                }
                public String call() throws
Exception {
                    Random random =
new Random();
                    Thread.sleep((random.
nextInt(20) * 100 + 100));
                    System.out.println("I
just arrived, waiting for the others...");
                    barrier.await();
                    System.out.println("L
et's go to the cinema!");
                    return "ok";
                }
        }
        ExecutorService executorService =
Executors.newFixedThreadPool(4);
```

```java
        CyclicBarrier barrier = new
CyclicBarrier(4, () ->
System.out.println("Barrier openning"));
        List<Future<String>> futures = new
ArrayList<>();
        try {
            for (int i = 0; i < 4; i++) {
                Friend friend = new
Friend(barrier);
                futures.add(executorServic
e.submit(friend));
            }
            futures.forEach(future -> {
                try {
                    future.get();
                } catch
(InterruptedException | ExecutionException
e) {
                    System.out.println(e.ge
tMessage());
                }
            });
        } finally {
            executorService.shutdown();
        }
    }
}
```

Output at console :
I just arrived, waiting for the others...
I just arrived, waiting for the others...
I just arrived, waiting for the others...
I just arrived, waiting for the others...
Barrier openning
Let's go to the cinema!
Let's go to the cinema!
Let's go to the cinema!
Let's go to the cinema!
The call method of the Callable interface is the
following. it will take a random time for a

friend to reach the cafe. When it arrives at the cafe, it just prints out this message, I just arrived and I'm waiting for the others, and then waiting for the others means call this barrier.await method. This method call is blocking until a set number of calls have been made on it. Once this number of call has been reached, the barrier opens and the code can continue, let's go to the cinema, and return ok. How are we going to use this code? Let us create an executor service on four threads, create a CyclicBarrier on the count of 4, and create 4 friends that's going to, of course, share the same barrier object. And we will submit those callables to the same executorService and accumulate the futures in this futures list. And then we are going to call the get method on each future and print out any message if there is an exception in the execution. Let us run this code. It executes as expected. All the four friends will arrive at random time at the cafe, and then when all those four friends are there together, they will go together to the cinema. Note that we can also pass a task to be executed just before the opening of the barrier. This task is, in fact, a runnable, so let us just print out a message Barrier Opening and execute the result. And indeed, this task has been executed just before the release of the thread that we're waiting on the await method.

Java Coding: Setting up the ExecutorService, Using TimeOut

So we just saw the cases when everything is okay. Now let us see how to undo exceptions and timeouts. Let us see our first case where things can go wrong. All the callables are executed in one given thread of our ExecutorService. This await method blocks those threads, but they do not release them. So if I have a count of 4 on a CyclicBarrier, I need to have at least 4 threads available in my Executor. If it is not the case, it means that this barrier will never open. Let us see that. Let us put two threads in this Executor. Change in previous class as shown below and run :

ExecutorService executorService = Executors.newFixedThreadPool(2);

Output at console :
I just arrived, waiting for the others...
I just arrived, waiting for the others...
The two first callable will be properly executed and will wait for the barrier to open, but since this Executor do not have any available threads for the two other tasks, they will never be executed and this barrier will never open. Now how can we handle the fact that this barrier is never going to open, or at least, will take a very long time, too much time to open properly. Well, this await method exists in several versions and there is one that takes a timeout as a parameter. Let us set this timeout to a high value like 5 SECONDS and see what happens.

Change in previous class as shown below and run :

```
barrier.await(5, TimeUnit.SECONDS);
```

Output at console :

I just arrived, waiting for the others...
I just arrived, waiting for the others...
java.util.concurrent.TimeoutException
java.util.concurrent.BrokenBarrierException
I just arrived, waiting for the others...
java.util.concurrent.BrokenBarrierException
I just arrived, waiting for the others...
java.util.concurrent.BrokenBarrierException

What we expect is the following. We have two tasks that are going to be properly executed, so this await method will be executed for them, but the two others are never going to be executed. So at some point, this await method will throw a timeout exception after 5 seconds. This timeout exception will be seen in this get method of the future and the barrier will be broken. Let us execute this code. So those are the two first tasks executed and you can see that a TimeoutException has been raised along with a BrokenBarrierException. In fact, the first task that timed out closed the other waiting task on the await method to throw this BrokenBarrierException. So those two tasks have failed. The two corresponding threads of our ExecutorService have been released and they became available to execute the two waiting tasks. So this is what we see here and when those two waiting tasks have reached the barrier and the await method, since the barrier was broken, that immediately threw this BrokenBarrierException. So here we saw two things, how to set a timeout on this await method. The first timeout to be reached will throw a TimeoutException that can be caught here in this get method. It will cause the barrier to break, so all of the other calls to this await method will immediately throw a BrokenBarrierException.

Java Coding: Using Future TimeOut and Task Cancellation

The second way of dealing with this is the following. We have removed the timeout from this await call and we can put another timeout on this future.get call here. Let us put it at 200 MILLISECONDS.
Change in previous class as shown below and run :

```
barrier.await();
futures.forEach(
                future -> {
                    try {
                        future.get(200,
TimeUnit.MILLISECONDS);

                    } catch
(InterruptedException | ExecutionException
e) {
                        System.out.printl
n(e.getMessage());
                    } catch
(TimeoutException e) {
                        System.out.printl
n("Timed out");
                    }
                }
            );
```

Output at console :
Timed out
Timed out

103

Timed out
Timed out
I just arrived, waiting for the others...
I just arrived, waiting for the others...
This version of the get method can throw a TimeoutException, so we are going to add a catch close to the surrounding try TimeoutException and here just print out Timed out. Let us run this code. Here we can see that our problem is only partially resolved. Why? Because all our future have timed out, so our main thread is not waiting for any result anymore. But our tasks are still waiting for the barrier to open and our two unexecuted tasks are still waiting in the ExecutorService, and we can see that here the JVM is still running because threads are still running in the ExecutorService executing tasks. So timing out this get method does not always cancel the running task, the corresponding running task, and in that case, it is only a partial solution. The proper way to handle this case completely with this solution is once this TimeoutException has been thrown, cancel the corresponding task by calling future.cancel and pass true since we want to interrupt the currently running tasks and the tasks waiting in the ExecutorService for an available thread.
Change in previous class as shown below and run :
future.cancel(true);
Output at console :
Timed out
Timed out
Timed out
Timed out
If we run this code as-is, it will work in the case that our application has exited properly,

so it means that the ExecutorService has been shut down and all the tasks have been cancelled, but if we want to see it more precisely, we need to surround this block of code with a try catch, catch the InterruptedException here, print out a message, Interrupted, for instance, and return nok.

Change in previous class as shown below and run :

```java
try {
                Random random =
new Random();
                Thread.sleep((random.
nextInt(20)*100 + 100));
                System.out.println("I
just arrived, waiting for the others...");

                barrier.await();

                System.out.println("L
et's go to the cinema!");
                return "ok";
        }
catch(InterruptedException e) {
                System.out.println("In
terrupted");
        }
                return "nok";
```

Output at console :
Timed out
Interrupted
Timed out
Interrupted
Timed out
Interrupted
I just arrived, waiting for the others...
Timed out
Interrupted

If we reach this point in the code, let us run this code again, and now we can see that each task is timed out and then interrupted by the cancel method call.

Java Coding Wrap-up

Let us quickly wrap up this Java coding session. What did we see in the code? Well, we saw how to create barriers with callbacks to have threads wait for each other on a certain condition. This is the role of the CyclicBarrier object. And we saw how to set a timeout on the CyclicBarrier.await call, how it works, by throwing a TimeoutException that we can catch on the future.get call, and how this could lead to a BrokenBarrierException. And we also saw how to set a timeout and a cancel on the Future.get call directly if a barrier takes too much time to open.

Module Wrap-up

Now is the time to wrap-up this third module of this book. What did we see? Well, we saw two tools to trigger an action on the completion of other actions. This is basically what we saw. The first of this tool is the CyclicBarrier. It is useful for parallel computations. It can trigger a callback task before open it and it can reset itself normally or can be reset exceptionally. And the second tool we saw is the CountDownLatch which is very useful for controlling the starting up of an application that depends on the proper initialization of collaborator services. This is the example that we saw. That's it for this module.

Module 4: Understanding Casing and Atomic Variables

Introduction, Module Agenda

Let us browse through the agenda. This module is all about CASing. Now what does CASing mean? In fact, it means compare and swap, and we are going to see what is it exactly because it is a notion that comes from the CPU from the assembly language and that is available in the JDK. We are going also to see why it is useful to use CASing and how it differs from synchronization, whether it is synchronization using classical synchronized blocks or locking using the lock interface. We are going to see how it has been implemented in the JDK, and what we can find in the JDK to implement CASing, and we would see how and when to use it.

Understanding Casing: Do We Always Need Synchronization?

- CASing = "Compare And Swap"

107

Let us first talk about CASing itself, that is compare and swap, and why it has been added to the CPU. The starting point is a set of assembly instructions that is very low level functionalities given by the CPU. Those low level functionalities have been exposed at the API level in the JDK on the many other languages so that we can leverage them in our applications. So what is CASing? Let us first state the problem. The problem it addresses is a classical concurrent programming problem that we saw in details. It is the concurrent access to shared memory. What does it mean? It means that several threads are trying to read and write, so read and modify the same variables of the same objects. Now the tools we have so far are synchronization tools, whether it is the classical synchronized block or the use of the lock interface. It works very well. It prevents several threads from modifying the same portion of memory at the same time. But in certain cases, we have more tools that would prove more efficient. In fact, synchronization has a cost and we can ask how ourselves the question, is it really always essential to use it. In fact, we use it to be sure that our code is correct. But if we didn't use it, are we really sure that our code would fail. In fact, there are many cases where people forget to synchronize the modification of memory and the code still works. What it means is that, in fact, there are many cases where real concurrency is rare.

Understanding Casing: An Example of False Concurrency

Let us examine a real problem of a portion of memory which access has been synchronized. We have a first thread T1 that reads a variable, suppose it is long, value is 10, and that we'll modify it. And then another thread is going to read it after that and modify it also. Here, we have a shared portion of memory. Since we want to be sure that this memory is correct, we have synchronized its success. But in fact, when our application is running, the thread T1 and T2 are not accessing this portion of memory at exactly the same time. They are accessing it one after another. So since we learn our concurrent stuff well and we know that we need to write correct code, we have used a synchronized block to protect this memory. This protection by lock is essential because if we do not do that and the two threads are writing and reading the code at exactly the same time, we will have concurrency issues race conditions. But in fact, when our application is running, there is no real concurrency at runtime because in the case we just saw, the thread T1 are not accessing this portion of memory at exactly the same time. And this is exactly the case where CASing precisely can be used.

Understanding Casing: How Does It Work?

How does CASing work? Well, this compare and swap stuff works with three parameters.

- Compare and Swap works with three parameters:
    - a location in memory
    - an existing value at that location
    - a new value to replace this existing value

The first is a location in memory, so basically, an address. The second parameter is the existing value supposedly written at this location. So this is the value we think should sit at that location. And the third is the new value that we want to write at that location. So this new value will replace the existing value. And the semantic is the following. If the current value at that address, that is the value that exists at that address, is the value we expect, then we replace it by the new value and returns true. It means that between the last time we read this address and now, no other thread has modified this location. If it is not the case, it means that between the last time we read this location and read the expected value and now, some of the thread has modified this location, so we are observing real concurrency. So since the expected value is not the value at that location, we do not do any modification and we return false. And all this comparison and modification are made uninterruptible, are made in a single atomic assembly instruction. So during this time, we are sure that no other thread can interrupt our process. This is essential for the CASing to work. So we can see that with such a functionality, we can modify values at given location in the memory without using synchronization, and if there is no real concurrency, as we saw in the previous example, it will be much more efficient than synchronization.

How to Use the AtomicLong Class and How Does It Work

Let us see an example of code with the AtomicLong class.
// Create an atomic long
AtomicLong counter = new AtomicLong(10L);
// Safely increment the value
long newValue=counter.incrementAndGet();
AtomicLong is a wrapper on a long. It can be used to create counters, so let us do that. We create an AtomicLong on the value 10 and we just increment and get this counter, which is a safe way of incrementing the value we have. So this pattern allows us to safely, in a concurrent way, increment the value of the counter without synchronization. What is happening under the hood? In fact, the Java API is going to try to apply the incrementation. The CASing implementation will tell the calling code if the incrementation failed or not. How can it fail? Well, it just fails if another thread modified the counter in the meantime. If the incrementation fails, then the API is going to try again until this incrementation is accepted by the CASing mechanism. So if we have several threads

incrementing the same counter, CASing ensures that no incrementation is lost. If we have 4 threads incrementing a counter 25 times, this counter will hold 100 as a value at the end of the day. The counter part is that more than 100 incrementations will be attempted most probably. Some of them will not be taken into account due to concurrency.

The Java Atomic API: The AtomicBoolean Class

So now that we saw the basic principles and some examples, let us browse through the API. We have several classes with different functionalities, whether this class is wrapping a Boolean, a number, or a reference. There are many methods in each of those classes and it makes things a little tedious, but I think it is still important to see that to have a good idea on how things have been designed and how they work. So we have at first the AtomicBoolean.

- AtomicBoolean :
  - get()
  - set()
  - getAndSet(value)
  - compareAndSet(expected, value)

What we can do on that, we can get and set the value, of course. This is a wrapper class, and we have this getAndSet method that will return the current value and update this value to the past value. And the last method is the compareAndSet, which is basically the CASing method with an expected value and the new value to be set if the expected value is matched.

The Java Atomic API: The AtomicInteger and AtomicLong Classes

- AtomicInteger, AtomicLong :
  - get()
  - set()
  - getAndSet(value)
  - compareAndSet(expected, value)
  - getAndUpdate(unaryOp)
  - updateAndGet(unaryOp)
  - getAndIncrement()
  - getAndDecrement()
  - getAndAdd(value)
  - addAndGet(value)
  - getAndAccumulate(value, binOp)
  - accumulateAndGet(value, binOp)

After that, we have the AtomicInteger and the AtomicLong to make counters, get and set value the same as previously, getAndSet method that takes a value, also the same kind of method, the compareAndSet method that takes the expected value and the new value we want to set, which is once again the exact implementation of the CASing, and we have more method that takes operators, getAndUpdate and updateAndGet. GetAndUpdate, of course, will return the current value and do the update. UpdateAndGet will do the contrary, first update, then get a new value. A unary operator may be implemented using the lambda expression and it is just an operation on the current value that will compute the new value. And we have more method, getAndIncrement and getAndDecrement. First, we tell the value, then do the modification. GetAndAdd and addAndGet which will increment the current value with the past value, the getAndAdd return the existing value and the addAndGet return the updated value. And the getAndAccumulate and accumulateAndGet, same kind of semantic that takes a binary operator. This binary operator will operate and the current value at that location and the past value as a parameter to compute the new value to be set in this AtomicInteger or AtomicLong.

The Java Atomic API: The AtomicReference Class

- AtomicReference<V>
  - get()
  - set()
  - getAndSet(value)
  - getAndUpdate(unaryOp)
  - updateAndGet(unaryOp)
  - getAndAccumulate(value, binOp)
  - accumulateAndGet(value, binOp)
  - compareAndSet(expected, value)

And then, the last Atomic class that exists is the AtomicReference. All the previous ones,

AtomicBoolean, AtomicInteger, and AtomicLong were wrappers on Java primitive types, Boolean, int, and long. This AtomicReference is a wrapper on the reference that is on a pointer. The set of method is almost the same. We have a get and set method, of course, getAndSet that takes a new value, getAndUpdate, that takes a unary operator. This unary operator operates on the type V, of course. GetAndAccumulate and accumulateAndGet, that takes a value and a binary operator built on the type V and the behavior is the same as the same method on integer and long. And the last one is compareAndSet with the expected value at that location and the new value to be set if the expected value matches the current value.

Wrapping-up the Atomic Objects

So one final word about CASing. CASing works well when concurrency is not too high. In fact, if the concurrency is high, then the update operation of the memory will be tried again and again until it is accepted by all the thread, and at one given point of time, only one thread will win. All the other ones will be retrying again and again. And the conclusion of that is that the behavior of a CASing system is very different from the behavior of a synchronized system. If you synchronize a portion of memory, it means that all your threads between are going to wait to access this memory. In the case of the CASing, all the threads at the same time are going to access this memory, but only one will be the winner. So if CASing is not used in the right use case,

115

it may create a very heavy load both on the memory and on the CPU. So let us do a little wrap up on Atomic variables. Atomic variables are based on CASing. CASing in another tool to handle concurrent read and write operation on memory. This tool works in a very different way than synchronization. It is not the same at all, and if it has been introduced, it is because it can lead to better performances. Now it should be used with care because in the case where the concurrency is very high, it will generate a heavy load on both the CPU and the memory.

Understanding Adders and Accumulators

Let us now talk about adders and accumulators. Adders and accumulators are an introduction of Java 8. These classes are not available in Java 7 and before. The starting point is a fact that all the methods we saw on Atomic variables are built on the modify and get or get and modify concept, and the fact is that sometimes we do not need the get part at each modification. Suppose we are just creating a counter and we just want to count a certain number of events, we want to make it in a thread-safe way so we are using an AtomicLong, for instance. Each time we increment this AtomicLong, we also get the current value of this Atomic Long, but the fact is we do not need this value at this time. All we need is the value once our process is done at the end of it. This is precisely the role of the LongAdder and the LongAccumulator classes introduced in Java 8. The LongAdder can be seen as an AtomicLong that does not expose the get functionality at each modification and that can optimize things.

Browsing Through the Adder and Accumulator API

So LongAdder and LongAccumulator work the same as an AtomicLong. The difference is that it does not return the updated value at each modification, so it can distribute the update on different cells if they are really many threads trying to do the modifications. And at the end of the day, when we call the get method, all the results from those different cells can be merged on that call. Those classes have been created to handle very high concurrency, a huge number of threads, it is quite useless to use them if it is not the case.

- LongAdder:
  - increment()
  - decrement()
  - add(long)
  - sum()
  - longValue()
  - intValue()
  - sumThenReset()

Let us browse through the methods we have on the LongAdder, increment and decrement. They do not return anything. Add, that takes long as a parameter. Sum, longValue, and IntValue, that's going to return the content of this LongAdder, and there is sumThenReset, that's where we return the content of this

LongAdder and reset the value to 0. And for the

- LongAccumulator:
  - built on a binary operator
  - accumulate(long)
  - get()
  - intValue()
  - longValue()
  - floatValue()
  - doubleValue()
  - getThenReset()

LongAccumulator, it is built on a binary operator since this is an accumulator, and then I can accumulate this longer. The current value and this past value will be used as parameters of this binary operator to produce a new value, and we have a get method to return the value computed in this accumulator. We also have a convenient method to convert this accumulated value in int, long, float, or double. And if we need to reset this accumulator while getting its value, we also have this getThenReset method.

Java Coding: Fixing a Race Condition on a Simple Counter

Now is the time for our little Java coding session. Let us see some code in action. What we're going to see here is some atomic counters in action, how we can use them, and how they work. Let us see now thread-safe counters in action using atomic variable. Let us first have a look at this very simple code.

```
package executors;
import java.util.ArrayList;
```

```java
import java.util.List;
import
java.util.concurrent.ExecutionException;
import java.util.concurrent.ExecutorService;
import java.util.concurrent.Executors;
import java.util.concurrent.Future;
public class AtomicCounter {
    private static int counter = 0;
    public static void main(String[] args) {
        class Incrementer implements
Runnable {
            public void run() {
                for (int i = 0; i < 1_000; i++)
{

                    counter++;
                }
            }
        }
        class Decrementer implements
Runnable {
            public void run() {
                for (int i = 0; i < 1_000; i++)
{

                    counter--;
                }
            }
        }
        ExecutorService executorService =
Executors.newFixedThreadPool(8);
        List<Future<?>> futures = new
ArrayList<>();
        try {
            for (int i = 0; i < 4; i++) {
                futures.add(executorServic
e.submit(new Incrementer()));
            }
            for (int i = 0; i < 4; i++) {
                futures.add(executorServic
e.submit(new Decrementer()));
```

```
            }
            futures.forEach(future -> {
                try {
                    future.get();
                } catch
(InterruptedException | ExecutionException
e) {
                        System.out.println(e.ge
tMessage());
                }
            });
            System.out.println("counter = "
+ counter);
        } finally {
            executorService.shutdown();
        }
    }
}
```

Here we have a counter, which is just an integer, private and static, and we have two classes implementing runnable that will increment the counter for the Increment Runnable and decrement this counter for the Decrementer Runnable. Each of this class does that 1,000 times, and what we are going to do now is just execute that in an ExecutorService of 8 threads we create for Incrementer and for Decrementer, execute them concurrently, wait for all those incrementers and decrementers to complete, and at the end of the day, just print out the results. Of course, there is a very huge race condition on this counter variable. This code has been made for that. So whereas, the result should be 0, there is very little chance that we reach 0 when execute this code. Let us run it and verify that, -500 and a few, - almost 700, -1,500. You see that even if we run this code several times, we do not have the same result, and if we run this code on your machine, there is very little chance that you get the same result as me. The first way we could use to make this code work is to lock everything to synchronize the excess of this incrementation and decrementation operation that would work without any problem, but we are going to do things differently by changing the type of this counter to AtomicInteger, so this counter is a new AtomicInteger of 0. Of course, we cannot use the ++ operator on this AtomicInteger. We have, for instance, incrementAndGet for the incrementation and decrementAndGet for the decrementation. Change the previous class as shown below and run :

```
private static AtomicInteger counter = new AtomicInteger(0);
counter.incrementAndGet();
counter.decrementAndGet();
```

Output at console :
counter = 0
And now if we were in the code, of course, the result is 0 and should be 0 on any kind of machine because we have made it completely thread-safe.

Java Coding: Counting the Number of Retries in an AtomicInteger

Let us see how this incrementation and the decrementation works under the hood, and for that, I modify the implementation of the counter we use to the MyCounter class, let us see that. This MyAtomicCounter class extends AtomicInteger.

```java
package executors;
import java.lang.reflect.Field;
import java.util.ArrayList;
import java.util.List;
import
java.util.concurrent.ExecutionException;
import java.util.concurrent.ExecutorService;
import java.util.concurrent.Executors;
import java.util.concurrent.Future;
import
java.util.concurrent.atomic.AtomicInteger;
import sun.misc.Unsafe;
public class AtomicCounter {
    private static class MyAtomicCounter
extends AtomicInteger {
        private static Unsafe unsafe = null;
        static {
            Field unsafeField;
            try {
                unsafeField =
Unsafe.class.getDeclaredField("theUnsafe");
                unsafeField.setAccessible(tr
ue);
                unsafe = (Unsafe)
unsafeField.get(null);
            } catch (Exception e) {
                e.printStackTrace();
            }
        }
        private AtomicInteger
countIncrement = new AtomicInteger(0);
        public MyAtomicCounter(int
counter) {
            super(counter);
        }

        public int myIncrementAndGet() {
            long valueOffset = 0L;
            try {
```

```java
            valueOffset =
unsafe.objectFieldOffset(AtomicInteger.class.
getDeclaredField("value"));
            } catch (NoSuchFieldException |
SecurityException e) {
                e.printStackTrace();
            }
            int v;
        do {
            v = unsafe.getIntVolatile(this,
valueOffset);

countIncrement.incrementAndGet();
        } while
(!unsafe.compareAndSwapInt(this,
valueOffset, v, v + 1));

        return v;
        }

        public int getIncrements() {
            return
this.countIncrement.get();
        }
    }

    private static MyAtomicCounter counter
= new MyAtomicCounter(0);
    public static void main(String[] args) {
        class Incrementer implements
Runnable {
            public void run() {
                for (int i = 0 ; i < 1_000 ;
i++) {
                    counter.myIncrement
AndGet();
                }
            }
        }
```

```java
class Decrementer implements
Runnable {
        public void run() {
            for (int i = 0 ; i < 1_000 ;
i++) {

                counter.decrementAnd
Get();
            }
        }
    }


    ExecutorService executorService =
Executors.newFixedThreadPool(8);
    List<Future<?>> futures = new
ArrayList<>();
    try {
        for (int i = 0 ; i < 4 ; i++) {
            futures.add(executorServic
e.submit(new Incrementer()));
        }
        for (int i = 0 ; i < 4 ; i++) {
            futures.add(executorServic
e.submit(new Decrementer()));
        }

        futures.forEach(
            future -> {
                try {
                    future.get();
                } catch
(InterruptedException | ExecutionException
e) {

                    System.out.printl
n(e.getMessage());
                }
            }
        );
```

```
            System.out.println("counter = "
+ counter);
            System.out.println("#
increments = " + counter.getIncrements());

        } finally {
            executorService.shutdown();
        }
    }
}
```

Output at console :

counter = 0

increments = 4404

It has this unsafe private static field here, initialized here. Now this block of code should absolutely not be added to any kind of application. It is just there for demonstration purposes, so do not do that in your application. And this myIncrementAndGet method is a modification of the incrementAndGet method of the AtomicInteger class. Basically, it is exactly the same method. The only difference is here I increment an internal counter called countIncrement and I can get the value of this countIncrement counter to count the number of times the incrementation of the internal value of this AtomicInteger fails. As we saw, incrementAndGet tries to increment the special location in the memory, and if this incrementation is made by two threads at the same time, the strategy is the following, one of the two threads will be able to do the incrementation and the other one will have to retry. This retry is just here, getIntVolatile of valueOffset, which is the location in memory, and compareAndSwapInt valueOffset of this location, v the expected value, and v+1 the new value bound to replace the previous 1.

Now if another thread is doing the same thing, v will not be the expected value at that location and this compareAndSwapInt will return false, thus triggering another try over the incrementation at that location. So the rest of the code is the same. We just print out the value of the counter at the end of this operation. Of course, it should still be 0, but we also print out the number of times the incrementation has been tried and retried. We have four incrementers. Each incrementer increments the counter 1,000 time, so the minimum number of retries is 4,000. Let us execute this code and we can see that it's much more than 4,000, nearly the double. We can execute this code several times and see that we do not have the same results at each run, which is perfectly normal, and you should not expect to have the same result on your machine neither if you run this code. So this shows the behavior of the AtomicInteger. Indeed, even if the concurrency is low, the AtomicInteger will have to retry the modification of the value it holds and it is the same for all the atomic variables we have in this Atomic API.

Java Coding Wrap-up

Let us do a quick wrap up on this Java coding session. What did we see? Well, we saw how to create an atomic counter in a thread-safe way without using synchronization and this is how basically all the atomic variables work in Java. And we also saw on this example that retrying should be expected. Relying on atomic operations leads to a very different behavior of our web application than relying on locked or synchronized operation retrying will occur. It can create a heavier load on both the memory on the CPU, so you really need to keep that in mind when designing concurrent systems.

Module Wrap-up

Time to wrap up the fourth module of this book about how to make variables. What did we learn here? Well, we see that when we need to update values or references in memory, CASing may be a better solution than locking. CASing is compare and swap. It is based on very efficient assembly instruction down to the CPU and it is, in some cases, more efficient than synchronization. We have several tools in this toolbox with common operations, basically AtomicBoolean, AtomicIntegers, and Longs, and AtomicReferences. We still need to choose the right tool for the job depending on many things, including the level of concurrency, but not only that. It is also good to know if our threads are updating location in memory at the same time or if it is not the case. And from that, we can choose between synchronization or Atomic variables. That's it for this fourth module of this book.

Module 5: Leveraging Concurrent Collections to

Simplify Application Design

Introduction, Module Agenda

The agenda of this module. We are going to talk about the Concurrent part of the Collection framework, namely concurrent collections and maps. As you know, there are two kinds of structures in the Collection Framework, first the collections themselves and then the maps. On the collection part, we have two concurrent structures, the Queue and the BlockingQueue, and on the map part, we have the ConcurrentMap, so we are going to cover all of these in this module. We will, of course, also cover the implementations and describe which one should be used and when, especially depending on the concurrency level of your application.

Implementing Concurrency at the API Level

Let us first talk about the notion of concurrent interfaces and why they have been added to the collection framework mainly in Java 5. Well, we saw in the previous modules of this book that it was possible to implement the Producer/Consumer pattern at the application level by dealing with concurrency inside our application and we used synchronized blocks of code or we used the lock interface to do that. The idea of those concurrent interfaces is to provide tools to implement that at the API level, that is to have API that are themselves, thread safe. For that, we need new definitions of interfaces of the Collection Framework and new implementations of those interfaces. We have two branches in the Collection Framework, the Collection branch and the Map branch, so we are going to see that in detail.

Hierarchy of Collection and Map, Concurrent Interfaces

So the Collection Framework has been released in Java 2 in 1998 with 4 interfaces for collection, Collection itself, List, Set, and SortedSet. In Java 5, 4 more interfaces have been added, Queue and Deque, which stands for double-ended queue, and two concurrent structures, BlockingQueue and BlockingDeque. In Java 6, the NavigableSet not concurrent has been added. And in Java 7, the TransferQueue, which is an extension of the BlockingQueue, has been added to the Collection Framework and it is indeed a concurrent structure. As for the map, the first version of the Collection Framework was released with maps and SortedMaps, not concurrent. In Java 5, the ConcurrentMap has been added. And in Java 6, NavigableMap, not concurrent, and ConcurrentNavigableMap, obviously, concurrent.

What Does It Mean for an Interface to Be Concurrent?

What does it mean to have concurrent interfaces? An interface in itself is not an implementation, so it cannot be inherently thread safe. In fact, being concurrent for an interface means that it defines a contract for concurrent environments. In the specification of its method, it tells that calling this method should be thread safe. And of course, the JDK provides implementations that follow these contracts. And if we want to implement those concurrent interfaces ourselves, we also have to follow those contracts. But concurrency is complex. And dealing with 10 threads is not the same as dealing with thousands of threads. So we need also different implementations, some of those are adapted for low-level concurrency and others adapted to very high-level concurrency.

Why You Should Avoid Vectors and Stacks

Let us begin by examining the concurrent lists of the Collection Framework. First of all, we have two classes, Vector and Stack, that are well-known classes and well-known for being thread safe. In fact, those classes are legacy structures from the early days of the JDK. They were there before the Collection Framework itself. It turns out that they are indeed thread safe, but very poorly, or at least, very basically implemented. If you check the source code of these classes, You will see in fact that all the methods are synchronized, so allowing for the basic level of concurrency when one thread is reading a vector, no other thread can access it, whether for read operations or write operations. So these structures should not be used anymore. If you are building a new application, do not use them, and if you are handling existing applications with vectors and stacks in them, you can consider removing them and replacing them with the new structures that we are going to see now.

Understanding Copy On Write Arrays

The first structure we are going to examine is the copy on write structure. This copy on write structure exists in two forms, one for lists and the other one for sets. Let us see how those structures are working. The nice thing is that it does not rely on any locking for read operations. So you can read a copy on write structure with any number of thread freely and in parallel. Write operations create, in fact, internally a copy of the existing structure and the new structure replaces the previous one by just moving a pointer from the old structure to the new one in a synchronized way. Let us see that in detail. A copy on write released, for instance, is built on an internal array with a pointer called Tab. This array cannot be modified, so all the read operations can be made in parallel and freely. Now if we want to add an element to this array, it will first create internally a copy of this array and add this element to this copy. All the threads that are currently reading the array are reading the previous version freely without seeing this new version. When this new version of the array is ready, we just move the top pointer from the previous version to the new one in a synchronized way. So the new read operations will see this new structure while there are other threads iterating over the previous one, they will not see the modification.

Wrapping up CopyOnWriteArrayList

So for copy on write structure, the thread that are already reading this Copy on Write object will continue to do so without seeing the modification. Whereas, the new threads, of course, will see the modification.

- Two structures:
  - CopyOnWriteArrayList
  - CopyOnWriteArraySet

We have two structures implementing this concept. The first one is the CopyOnWriteArrayList. It is an implementation of list with a semantic of list, and the CopyOnWriteArraySet, which is an implementation of set, thus with a semantic of a set. These Copy on Write Structures obviously work very well when you have many reads and very, very few writes, very few modifications of the array. If you have many writes, it mean that you will have many copies of the array, which is costly. There are use cases very well adapted to this structure. For instance, if you want to store parameters for your application during the initialization phase of your application, then you can do so in a thread-safe way, and when your application is initialized, you are not going to touch these parameters again, so you can distribute this Copy on Write array anywhere you want in a thread-safe way.

Introducing Queue and Deque, and Their Implementations

Let us see now the second type of structures available, queues and stacks. And when I say stack, I do not mean the Stack class, but of course, the stack concept.
- Queue and Deque: interfaces
- ArrayBlockingQueue: a bounded blocking queue built on an array
- ConcurrentLinkedQueue: an unbounded blocking queue

We have two interfaces to deal with that called queue and deque. Deque stands for double-ended queue and it can be seen as a queue that can be accessed from both the head and the tail. We have a first implementation called ArrayBlockingQueue as we're going to see. It is a bounded blocking queue built on an array. Bounded means that we create a blocking queue with a certain amount of cells, a certain size of the array, and once this queue is full, it does not extend itself. Adding elements to it would not be possible. And we have the ConcurrentLinkedQueue. It is an unbounded blocking queue in which we can add as many elements as we need. How does a queue work? We all know that we have two kinds of queues in computer science, the FIFO, First In First Out, which is the queue itself, and the LIFO, Last In First Out, which is the stack. In the JDK, they are modeled by the following, the queue is the interface for the Queue and the Deque is the interface for both a queue and a stack. In fact, we do not have a pure stack in the JDK, that is an interface that model a stack without modeling also a queue. We do not count the Stack class since, once again, you should not use this class.

Understanding How Queue Works in a Concurrent Environment

Suppose our queue is built on an array. The producer will add element from the tail and the consumer will consume them from the head. So we have several elements in our queue. Those elements are going to be consumed one by one by the consumer. But we are in a concurrent world. We can have as many producers and as many consumers as we need, and of course, each of them is in its own thread, so our queue or deque will be accessed in a concurrent way. Of course, a thread does not know in advance how many elements there are in the queue or in a stack and querying a concurrent structure for the number of elements it has is not such a good idea because between the time we query that and the time where we use this information, this information might have changed dramatically. So this raises two questions. First, what happens if the queue or the stack is full and we need to add an element to it, and if you remember what we did to implement that using the lock interface, you might remember that we called the wait or the await method on the thread. And second question, what happens if the queue or the stack is empty and we need to get an element from it.

Adding Elements to a Queue That Is Full: How Can It Fail?

Suppose we want to add an element to a queue that is full. This might occur with the ArrayBlockingQueue. Of course, it will not occur with the ConcurrentLinkedList Queue since this ConcurrentLinkedList queue can adapt its internal size to the number of elements it has to hold.
boolean add(E e); // fail: IllegalArgumentException
// fail: return false
boolean offer(E e); boolean offer(E e, timeOut, timeUnit);
// blocks until a cell becomes available
voidput(E e);

The first behavior is we should fail it with an IllegalArgumentException and this is the behavior of the add method. In fact, if we try to add an element using this method, it will fail with an exception, but there are other ways of dealing with this. We also call the offer method, which is another method, and this method will return false instead of throwing this IllegalArgumentException. Another way of telling the calling thread that adding an element is not possible, and if the queue is a BlockingQueue and this is the semantic of the blocking part of the BlockingQueue, we can also try to put an element in this queue and this call will block until a cell becomes available. We even have a fail behavior which is an offer call with a timeout. Here, we are saying okay I want to add this element in the queue and I'm okay to wait for let's say 100 ms to do so. If passed that time this element has not been added, then I prefer to fail and to do so by returning a false value. So we can see that adding an element to a queue can be made in three ways plus one. It can fail with an exception, fail with a special value, returned, which is here Boolean, or block until a cell becomes available. So this is the basic way of things are working and we will have the same for all the operations available on the queue and the deque.

Understanding Error Handling in Queue and Deque

So in a nutshell, for the addition of an element at the Tail of the Queue, we have two behaviors.
- Two behaviors:
  - Failing with an exception
  - Failing and returning false
- And for blocking queue:
  - Blocking until the queue can accept the element

We can fail with an exception, we can fail by returning false, and if the queue is a blocking queue, we can block until the queue can accept the element. But we also have Deque and BlockingDeque.

- Deque : addFirst(), offerFirst()
- BlockingDeque : putFirst()

Deque can accept elements at the head of a queue with the method addFirst and offerFirst. And in a case of a BlockingDeque, putFirst, and the add offer and put behaviors are the same as the behaviors that we just saw that is fail with an exception, fail by returning false, and block until a cell is available. But we are not quite done. We also have the get and peek operation.

- Queue:
  - Returns null: poll() and peek()
  - Exception: remove() and element()
- BlockingQueue:
  - blocks: take()

Get is to remove an element from a queue and peek is just to examine an element without removing it from the queue. So for the queue poll and peek return null. Remove and element will throw exceptions. And for the BlockingQueue, take will block until an element is available. And for the deque, returns null for pollLast and peekLast, exception for removeLast and getLast, and in a case of a BlockingDeque, takeLast will block until an element is available.

Wrapping up Queue, Deque, and Their Blocking Versions

So for Queue and BlockingQueue, we have four different types of queues, they may be blocking or not, and they may offer access from both sides or not, so that makes four types of queue. We have a different type of failure, fail with a special value, here a Boolean, fail with an exception, or block until the operation is possible. So all these make the API quite complex. We have a lot of methods in it. The JDK is well organized on this point. If you check the JavaDoc of Queue, BlockingQueue, Deque, and BlockingDeque, you will have tables with a nice summary of all these methods.

Introducing Concurrent Maps and Their Implementations

Let us see now the concept of concurrent maps. In fact, we have only one interface, ConcurrentMap, which is an extension of the map interface. The object of this ConcurrentMap is not to add any new method to the map interface, but merely to redefine the JavaDoc of those methods. We have two implementations of ConcurrentMap. The first is the ConcurrentHashMap. There is one available up to JDK 7, and in JDK 8, it has been completely we return. We are going to see that. And the ConcurrentSkipListMap introduced in Java 6, which does not rely on any synchronization. We are also going to see this structure in details.

Atomic Operations Defined by the ConcurrentMap Interface

Besides being thread safe, ConcurrentMap also defines atomic operations. They are for them.

- putIfAbsent(key, value)
- remove(key, value)
- replace(key, value)
- replace(key, existingValue, newValue)

The first one is the putIfAbsent that takes a key and a value and that will add this key value pair to the map if the key is not already present in the map. This putIfAbsent is atomic in the sense that between the instant where the presence of the key is checked in the map and the adding of this key value pair, no other thread can interrupt this method. The same goes for the version of remove that takes a key and a value. This key value pair will be removed from the map if it is present. It is in fact the equivalent of remove if present. There is no interruption possible between the instant where the thread checks for the presence of the key in the map associated with the right value and the instance where the remove is performed. And then we have two last methods, the first one is replace that takes a key and value and that will replace the value currently associated with that key with this new value and the replace key, existingValue, and newValue that will replace existing value by new value if existingValue is already associated with that key in this map. Those two replace methods cannot be interrupted between the checking of the presence of the key in the map and the replacement of the value.

Understanding Concurrency for a HashMap

Now let us take a closer look at the implementations and let us try to understand what is at stake with this implementation. We need implementations that are thread safe, efficient up to a certain number of threads, and we are going to see that this is a key point in dealing with maps, and a number of efficient, parallel special operations, and this is offered by the ConcurrentHashMap from Java 8. How does a hashmap work internally? This is important to understand to understand also concurrency. In the JDK, a hashmap is built on an array. When I want to add the key value pair to this array, first I compute a hashcode from the key. This hashcode will decide which cell of this array will hold the key value pair, and when this is done, a pointer will point from this cell to this value pair. So if I have two key value pairs in my hashmap, this structure will be the following. Note that each cell is called a bucket and a bucket can hold several key value pairs since different keys may have the same hashcode. So adding a key value pair to a map is a several steps problem. First, we need to compute the hashcode of the key. Second, we need to determine which cell of the array will hold this key value pair and we first need to check the bucket has been created or not. If it's not, then we create it and add the key value pair to it, pretty straightforward. If there is already a bucket, we need to check if this bucket is already holding this same key or not. If it is the case, then the value we try to add will replace the existing value. If it is not, there is a special process that is launched. In the hashmap, it will create a link list up to a certain number of key value pairs and will switch to a red-black tree past this number. This is the full step, the updating of the map. In a concurrent world, all these steps must not be interrupted by any other thread because if it is the case, it will just corrupt the map by corrupting either the bucket, either the linked list, either the red-black tree.

Understanding the Structure of the ConcurrentHashMap from Java 7

So how are we going to do that? We know that the only way to make array-based operation thread safe, that is to guard an array-based structure, is to lock the array, and there is no way in Java we can lock only portions of the array. Either we lock all the way, either we do not lock it at all. Synchronizing the put operation will work, but it would be extremely inefficient because it would block all the map. What we would want to do is to allow several threads to work on different buckets concurrently, that is to allow concurrent reads on the map. If we synchronize all the map, it means that we need to synchronize the array itself. It will work, no doubt about that, but it will be very inefficient because it will block everything, even the read operations on the map itself. What we could do is segment the array in several subarrays and synchronize on each segment. The nice thing, once again, is that it works and it allows for a certain level of parallelism. As long as all the threads work on each individual segment, I can have concurrent reads and even concurrent writes. And this is exactly the organization of the ConcurrentHashMap up to JDK 7. It is built on a set of synchronized segment. The number of segments is called the concurrency level. By default, it is set to 16 and it can be set up to 64,000. This sets number of threads that can access this map concurrency, but we need to keep in mind that the number of key value pairs has to be greater than the concurrency level and I would say much greater than the concurrency level. If the number of key value pairs is lesser than the concurrency level, then the limit is not the concurrency level, but the number of key value pairs.

Introducing the Java 8 ConcurrentHashMap and Its Parallel Methods

Let us now take a closer look at this ConcurrentHashMap from Java 8. As I said, the implementation of the ConcurrentHashMap has completely changed between Java 7 and Java 8. It is still compatible from the serialization point of view. It means that if you have a serialized Java 7 ConcurrentHashMap, you can deserialize it as a ConcurrentHashMap from Java 8 and vice versa. It has been created to handle very heavy concurrency, thousands of threads, and millions of key value pairs, and because of that, some more methods not defined on map or ConcurrentMap have been added with parallel implementations.

Parallel Search on a Java 8 ConcurrentHashMap

Let us see that now.
ConcurrentHashMap<Long, String>map= ...;
// JDK 8
String result =
    map.search(10000,
        (key, value) -
    >value.startsWith("a") ? "a": null
    );
The ConcurrentHashMap, for instance, has a method for parallel searching of key value pairs. The first parameter passed to this search method is called the parallelism threshold and the second one is the operation to be applied. If this operation returns a non-null value, this value will be returned by the search method and it will stop the exploration of the map. We also have other search methods, searchKeys, searchValues, and searchEntries. Now what is this parallelism threshold? It is the number of key value pairs in this map that will trigger a parallel search. In our case, if we have more than 10,000 key

143

value pairs in this map, this search will be conducted in parallel.

Parallel Map / Reduce on a Java 8 ConcurrentHashMap

```
ConcurrentHashMap<Long,
List<String>>map= ...; // JDK 8
String result =
        map.reduce(10_000,
                (key, value) -> value.size(),
                (value1, value2) ->
                Integer.max(value1, value2)
        );
```

We also have a reduce method. The first bifunction maps each key value pair to an element that will be used for reduction, and the second bifunction, it is the reduction itself. It takes two elements returned by this mapping bifunction and reduce those two elements together. Of course, this second bifunction should be associative as in all reduction operation. And once again, this reduce method takes a parallel threshold, that is if we have more than 10,000 key value pairs in this map, this reduction will be conducted in parallel.

Parallel ForEach on a Java 8 ConcurrentHashMap

```
ConcurrentHashMap<Long,
List<String>>map= ...; // JDK 8
String result =
```

144

```
map.forEach(10_000,
        (key, value) -> value.removeIf(s-
> s.length() > 20)
    );
```

And the last parallel method available on this ConcurrentHashMap in Java 8 is the forEach method. The first parameter is also a parallelism threshold, so here if we have more than 10,000 key value pairs, this forEach operation will be computed in parallel. And the second and main parameter is a biconsumer that takes a key value pair and does something. This biconsumer is applied to all the key value pairs of the map. Here, what does it do? The value is a list of string, so on all the values of the map, we will remove all the strings that are longer than 20 characters. We also have other versions of this forEach method, forEachKeys that takes a consumer of key, forEachValues that takes a consumer values, and forEachEntry that takes a consumer of entry, which is the object that model the key value pair.

Creating a Concurrent Set on a Java 8 ConcurrentHashMap

```
Set<String>set=
ConcurrentHashMap.<String>newKeySet(); //
JDK 8
```

We do not have concurrent hash set in the JDK, but we have a static factory method on the ConcurrentHashMap from JDK 8 called newKeySet that will create a set here, a set of string backed by this ConcurrentHashMap. So this ConcurrentHashMap can also be used as a concurrent set with the same kind of semantics. Note that the parallel operations of the ConcurrentHashMap are not available on this set. In fact, the implementation of this set is a public static class defined as a member of this ConcurrentHashMap with no parallel operations defined on it.

Wrapping up the Java 8 ConcurrentHashMap

Let us do a quick wrap up on this ConcurrentHashMap. First, it is a fully concurrent map, which is nice. It has been made to handle very high concurrency and millions of key value pairs. It exposes built-in parallel operations, which is very nice. Those operations are not present in the map or concurrent map, and it can also be used to create very efficient and very large concurrent sets.

Introducing Skip Lists to Implement ConcurrentMap

And the last structure I would like to show you in this module is the concurrent skip list. As we saw the concurrent skip list is used for two implementations in the JDK. It is another concurrent map introduced in JDK 6. It is based on a structure called a skip list. Now what is a skip list? A skip list is a smart structure used to create linked lists and to provide fast random access to any of its elements. The concurrent version of this skip list implemented in Java 6 relies on atomic reference operations and no synchronization is used in it making it a very efficient structure even in a high concurrency environment and it is used in the JDK to create both maps and sets.

Understanding How Linked Lists Can Be Improved by Skip Lists

What is a skip list? Let us start with a classical linked list.

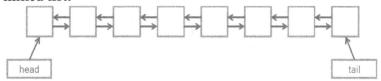

The representation of a linked list with a pointer to the head and another pointer to the tail of this linked list. The problem of a linked list is that it takes a very long time to reach randomly an element of this list. We say that the complexity is in big O of N meaning that if I double the number of elements of the linked list, I also double the mean access time to any of its elements.

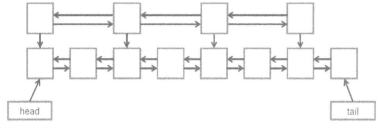

The solution this skip lists brings is to create a fast access list with less elements on top of it.

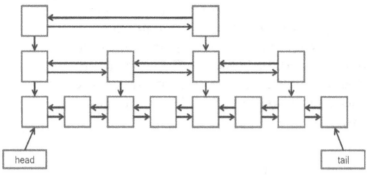

We can even create several layer of such a fast access list, in fact, as many as we need. The use of those fast access lists assume that the elements of the skip list are sorted. Now in fact, since it is a list, we can always store key value pairs in the form of Index object and sort those key value pairs using the index. So it is always possible to do that on the list.

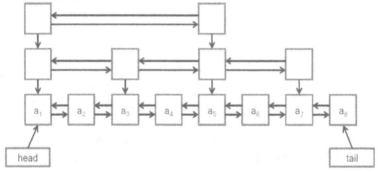

And now, the access time, instead of being big O of N, becomes big O of log of N, meaning that if I have a million elements in my skip list, instead of having an average access time in the order of a million, I will have an average access time in the order of 20, which is, of course, much, much faster. Let us see that on an example.

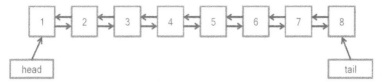

Suppose I have integers in my list sorted in their natural order.

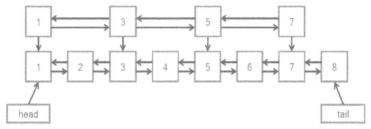

We create a first layer of fast access by just selecting elements from the skip list, one out of two. The creation of this layer is handled internally by the API and is completely transparent for me as a developer.

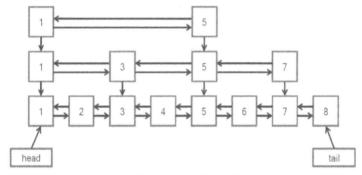

I can create a second layer with half of the elements. And now, suppose I need to locate the fourth element and probably the object linked to that index, what I need to do is check the first layer.

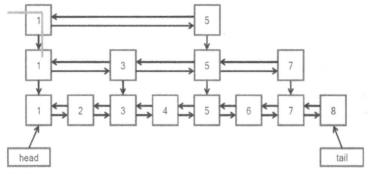

Notice that 4 is between 1 and 5, so I go down one floor on the first element.

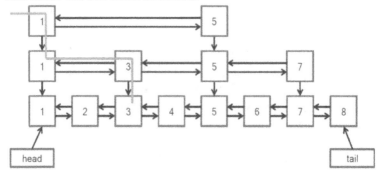

Then the 4 is between 3 and 5, so I go down 1 floor on the third element and then reach the fourth in only 3 steps.

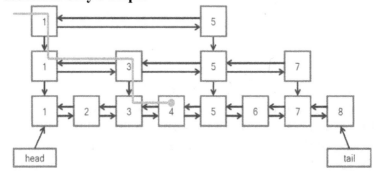

Wrapping up the Skip List Structure

So a skip list can be used both to implement linked list and also maps, as long as the keys are comparable objects, but most of the time, it is the case. The skip list structure is there to ensure fast random access to any key and a skip list is not an array-based structure, which is very nice because we saw that on array-based structure we have to synchronize on all the array itself and we cannot synchronize on portions of the array. So since it is not an array-based structure, we can imagine other ways than locking to guard a skip list, that is to make this skip list thread safe.

How to Make a Skip List Concurrent Without Synchronization

In a JDK, we have two implementations that use this structure. The first one is the ConcurrentSkipListMap, which is a map. All the references in this skip list are implemented using AtomicReference. In fact, if we check the skip list precisely, we see that all the operations are operations and pointers on references, so it can be implemented using this, and this is the trick used to make this skip list thread safe. This map is, of course, thread safe. It does not use synchronization at all, so it can be used in very high concurrency environment. We also have another implementation, which is an implementation of a set interface called the ConcurrentSkipListSet that uses the same structure as the ConcurrentSkipListMap. Both structures can be used in high concurrency environment as long as there are enough elements in it.

Wrapping up ConcurrentSkipList

So let us wrap up this part on concurrent skip lists. They can be used for both maps and sets. Thread safety is achieved without relying on locking, that is on synchronization, it is usable when concurrency is high, as long as there are enough elements in those lists. As usual, some methods should not be used on this kind of structure, namely the size method call. Never call size on the concurrent map or on a concurrent collection.

Java Coding: Producer / Consumer Built on an ArrayBlockingQueue

Okay, now it's time for a little Java coding session. Let us see some code in action. We are going to see an implementation of a Consumer/Producer pattern using an ArrayBlockingQueue and you will see that it may be much simpler than what we saw with the lock interface or the synchronize block, and we are going to see also the ConcurrentHashMap from Java 8 in action on parallel operations. Now that we have this BlockingQueue available, let us take a look at a Producer/Consumer pattern implemented using this structure.

```java
package executors;
import java.util.ArrayList;
import java.util.List;
import java.util.concurrent.ArrayBlockingQueue;
import java.util.concurrent.BlockingQueue;
import java.util.concurrent.Callable;
import java.util.concurrent.ExecutionException;
import java.util.concurrent.ExecutorService;
import java.util.concurrent.Executors;
import java.util.concurrent.Future;
public class ProducerConsumer {
    public static void main(String[] args)
throws InterruptedException {
        BlockingQueue<String> queue =
new ArrayBlockingQueue<>(50);

        class Consumer implements
Callable<String> {
            public String call() throws
InterruptedException {
                int count = 0;
                while (count++ < 50) {
                    queue.take();
                }
                return "Consumed " +
(count - 1);
            }
        }
        class Producer implements
Callable<String> {
            public String call() throws
InterruptedException {
                int count = 0;
```

```java
                    while (count++ < 50) {
                        queue.put(Integer.toSt
ring(count));
                    }
                    return "Produced " +
(count - 1);
                }
            }
        List<Callable<String>>
producersAndConsumers = new
ArrayList<>();
        for (int i = 0; i < 2; i++) {
            producersAndConsumers.add(n
ew Producer());
        }
        for (int i = 0; i < 2; i++) {
            producersAndConsumers.add(n
ew Consumer());
        }

        System.out.println("Producers and
Consumers launched");
        ExecutorService executorService =
Executors.newFixedThreadPool(4);
        try {
            List<Future<String>> futures =
executorService.invokeAll(producersAndCons
umers);
                futures.forEach(future -> {
                    try {
                        System.out.println(fut
ure.get());
                    } catch
(InterruptedException | ExecutionException
e) {
                        System.out.println("E
xception: " + e.getMessage());
                    }
                });
```

```
        } finally {
              executorService.shutdown();
              System.out.println("Executor
service shut down");
         }
     }
}
```

Output at console :
Producers and Consumers launched
Produced 50
Produced 50
Consumed 50
Consumed 50
Executor service shut down

You can see that the new Consumer class is much simpler than the previous one. Basically, we do not need any more synchronization, anymore lock, anymore wait/notify, or await/signal pattern, whatever. All we have to create is a BlockingQueue, for instance, or a queue implemented with an ArrayBlockingQueue of capacity 50. Then the consumer takes element from the BlockingQueue. This take method will block until an element is available. On the producing side, the producer puts an element in the queue. We set all that in an ExecutorService, get the futures, and print out the results. Let us run this code plain and simple. It just works as intended, but with a much more simple code. The JavaDoc of the BlockingQueue was really worth checking to get a summary of all the methods there are. I have here the three kinds of operation, insert, remove, and examine, which are the three basic operation on a queue and the behaviors of those operations through an exception return a special value blocks and times out depending on the type of operation that makes

155

quite a lot of different methods. Now these number of methods has to be multiplied by two for the deque interface, double-ended queue interface. This set of methods is only for the BlockingQueue interface. By the way, here is the equivalent tables for the deque. Here the summary of the deque method, the comparison of the queue and deque methods, and the comparison of the stack and deque method in the JavaDoc.

Java Coding: Parallel ForEach in Action on a ConcurrentHashMap

ConcurrentHashMap has been a very popular data structure these days. Java 8 introduced the forEach, search, and reduce methods, which are pretty much to support parallelism.

```
package executors;
import
java.util.concurrent.ConcurrentHashMap;
public class
ConcurrentHashMapParallelPatterrns {
    public static void main(String[] args) {
        ConcurrentHashMap<String,
Integer> hashMap = new
ConcurrentHashMap<>();
        hashMap.put("A", 1);
        hashMap.put("B", 2);
        hashMap.put("C", 3);
        hashMap.put("D", 4);
        hashMap.put("E", 5);
        hashMap.put("F", 6);
        hashMap.put("G", 7);
        hashMap.forEach(2, (k, v) ->
System.out.println(
```

```
            "key->" + k + "is related
with value-> " + v + ", by thread-> " +
Thread.currentThread().getName()));
        }
}
```
Output at console :
key->Ais related with value-> 1, by thread->
main
key->Dis related with value-> 4, by thread->
ForkJoinPool.commonPool-worker-2
key->Bis related with value-> 2, by thread->
main
key->Eis related with value-> 5, by thread->
ForkJoinPool.commonPool-worker-2
key->Cis related with value-> 3, by thread->
main
key->Fis related with value-> 6, by thread->
ForkJoinPool.commonPool-worker-2
key->Gis related with value-> 7, by thread->
ForkJoinPool.commonPool-worker-2
ParallelismThreshold is to define how you
wanted to execute the operations —
sequentially or in parallel. Suppose you have
given a parallelismThreshold as 2. So as long
as there are fewer than two elements in your
map, it would be sequential. Otherwise, it's
parallel (depends on the JVM).
It produced the above o/p on my machine (you
can see two different threads in action — main
and ForkJoinPool.commonPool-worker-1)

Java Coding: Parallel Search in
Action on a ConcurrentHashMap

package executors;

```java
import
java.util.concurrent.ConcurrentHashMap;
public class
ConcurrentHashMapParallelPatterrns {
    public static void main(String[] args) {
        ConcurrentHashMap<String,
Integer> hashMap = new
ConcurrentHashMap<>();
        hashMap.put("A", 1);
        hashMap.put("B", 2);
        hashMap.put("C", 3);
        hashMap.put("D", 4);
        hashMap.put("E", 5);
        hashMap.put("F", 6);
        hashMap.put("G", 7);
        String result = hashMap.search(1,
(k, v) ->
{           System.out.println(Thread.current
Thread().getName());
                if (k.equals("A"))
                    return k + "-" + v;
                return null;
        });
        System.out.println("result => " +
result);
    }
}
```

Output at console :
main
ForkJoinPool.commonPool-worker-1
ForkJoinPool.commonPool-worker-2
result => A-1

Java Coding: Computing an Reduce on a ConcurrentHashMap

```java
package executors;
import java.util.concurrent.ConcurrentHashMap;
public class ConcurrentHashMapParallelPatterrns {
    public static void main(String[] args) {
        ConcurrentHashMap<String, Integer> reducedMap = new ConcurrentHashMap<>();
        reducedMap.put("One", 1);
        reducedMap.put("Two", 2);
        reducedMap.put("Three", 3);
        System.out.println("reduce example => " + reducedMap.reduce(2, (k, v) -> v * 2, (total, elem) -> total + elem));
        System.out.println("reduceKeys example => " + reducedMap.reduceKeys(2,
                (key1, key2) ->
        key1.length() > key2.length() ? key1 + "-" + key2 : key2 + "-" + key1));
        System.out.println("reduceValues example => " + reducedMap.reduceValues(2,
        (v) -> v * 2,
                (value1, value2) -> value1 > value2 ? value1 - value2 : value2 - value1));
        System.out.println("After reduce => " + reducedMap);
    }
}
Output at console :
reduce example => 12
reduceKeys example => Three-Two-One
reduceValues example => 0
```

159

After reduce => {One=1, Two=2, Three=3}

Java Coding Wrap-up

Let us now wrap up this Java coding session
quickly. What did we see in this Java coding
session? Well, we saw two things, first another
producer/consumer implementation, but this
time relying on concurrent queues and no
locking, no synchronization whatsoever. The
pattern was extremely simple and I also
showed you where you could find the magic
tables to find your ways in the many methods
of concurrent queue and double-ended queue.
And at last, we saw the ConcurrentHashMap
parallel operations in action.

Module Wrap-up

Now is the time to wrap up this module. What
did we learn? Well, we saw that the JDK has
many things to offer on the concurrent
collections and maps front. Those structures
can be used to solve concurrent problems with
delegating thread safety to the API. This is
especially the case for the queue and the
double-ended queue, but also the case for skip
lists and concurrent maps. We focused a little
on blocking queues and concurrent maps
because blocking queues are really specific in
the concurrent field with the queue and the
double-ended queue and all the methods and
behaviors it offers and on ConcurentHashMap
from Java 8 because of the parallel operation
it offers. Now you may also ask yourself which

structure should I use in my application. That is, which structure for which case. In fact, if there is one answer to keep in mind, it is the following. There is no silver bullet in this field. If you have very few writes, and especially, very few writes passed a certain period of time, namely the initialization of your application, then you might consider using the copy and write structures, which are basically immutable structures. If you have low concurrently, really any solution will do, and you can rely on synchronization. If you are in a high concurrency context, skip lists are usable as long as there are many object in them and you can always rely on the ConcurrentHashMap, which works very well in this case. And if you have high concurrency with few objects, then you are in the problematic area of concurrency. If you rely on synchronization, you will block your threads. If you rely on atomic references or atomic variable, you will generate high CPU load and high memory load.

Book Wrap-up

It is also time to wrap up this book, so just a few words of advice to conclude this book. Be careful when designing concurrent code. First of all, you need to be sure to have a good idea of what your problem is. Second, you need to keep in mind that concurrent programming is different from parallel processing, in fact, it has nothing to do. Third, try to delegate the API as much as you can. And fourth, know the concurrent collection well because they can bring many solutions to your problem. You have the queues, you have the immutable structures, this key place, and the ConcurrentHashMap. And that's it for this book.

www.ingramcontent.com/pod-product-compliance
Lightning Source LLC
La Vergne TN
LVHW051240050326
832903LV00028B/2481